OpenERP evaluation with SAP as reference

Learn by discovering where the challenger meets the leader.

This publication consists of the opinions of FERIDIS organization based on researches and years of experience in the ERP world and should not be construed as statements of fact. The opinions expressed herein are subject to change, and a Twitter (@FERIDIS_COM[1]) and FACEBOOK account[2] have been created to discuss on the topic.

---

[1] http://twitter.com/FERIDIS_COM
[2] http://www.facebook.com/feridis.com

Acknowledgment

The article we have planned ended up being a book …

We would like to thank all the people who have encouraged us and who have given their time to review the book content.

About Us

Dealing for 15 years with clients' business needs in the Big Four companies, our policy has always been and still is a customer centric approach. This approach consists in offering a solution that fits the needs, timeline and budget of the clients. A solution that can be easily integrated in the IT landscape and accepted by the end-users and that will evolve at the same time with the company.

Our mission is to support clients to improve their business performances and profitability through the implementation of SAP's ERP, Business Intelligence environments and Process Management systems in a wide range of industry sectors such as the Telecommunication, Professional Services, Transportation & Logistics, Metals, European Institutions, Cargo airline, Retail, Manufacturing, Banking, etc

These projects consist of implementing the technology as well as the processes and the organizational changes necessary for success. They are characterised by:

- Budget between 1 M€ and 12M€;
- Size between 200 and 1500 users;
- Geographical scope from local to global; and
- Technologies such as SAP, Microsoft Dynamics, OpenERP, etc.

Preface of the authors

One day I showed OpenERP to a former boss of mine in one of the Big Four companies. He was really enthusiastic over the presentation. When I asked him his opinion, he said to me: "Yves, this is incredible! I see the same opportunity with OpenERP that the one I perceived when I discovered SAP R/2 in 1988".

While discussing with him and with my SAP network as well, we were asked the same questions over and over again: «What are the functionalities covered by OpenERP?", "How much does it cost?", "What does open source mean?", "Is it difficult to implement?", "What is the technology behind?", "What is the viability of the tool?", "Is there any support?", "What kind of hardware does it require?", "How is the workflow set up?", etc. In short, they all wanted to know the maturity of the product compared to their point of reference: SAP, leader on the market.

Convinced by the solution and the opportunities it offers and wishing to share our knowledge, we have decided to write this book for your attention whether you are a decision maker, an ERP client or an ERP player.

This book will help you to go beyond your convictions and open your imagination to what could be the management tool of tomorrow. As Albert Einstein said, "Imagination is more important than knowledge".

A world in constant evolution

The first "industrial" application of the electricity appeared around 1880 when a steam generator had been connected to an alternator. The electricity produced was used to light the production lines and increase the production capacity and quality thanks to a better lighted work environment. Some 20 people worked on the electricity power environment in order to produce the company lighting. When the electricity transport began in the 1890s, the power production was localized in very restricted area. The world had to wait until 1920 to get an "industrial" electricity network. In 1955, in the U.K., the first nuclear power unit produced 9 MW of electricity a day. Nowadays, a nuclear power unit can produce more than 1500 MW a day. From the isolated steam generator to the 1500 MW power units, 130 years have gone by.

Computers were born around 1935 with the electromagnetism pieces (relays). The first computer, the IBM 601, was able to calculate some basic operations with a really limited computing power: 1 multiplication per second. 1500 units of this computer were produced for the accounting and scientific sectors. According to IBM, the first real computer was created in 1948. It appeared in companies in 1956 and in houses in 1984.

The first Enterprise Resource Planning (ERP)[3] concept was born in the early 1960s from a joint effort between a construction machinery manufacturer and IBM. This application software was used as a method for planning and scheduling materials for complex manufactured products. In 1972, five former employees of IBM have decided to create a new company called "Systems Applications and Products in data processing" in order to develop a new kind of ERP. In 1976, the company was renamed "SAP GmbH". The first R/1 version was launched in 1973. Six years later, SAP launched the R/2 release; and the R/3 release, in 1992.

---

3 See definition in annex

The vision of SAP was the centralisation of the information to remedy the IT

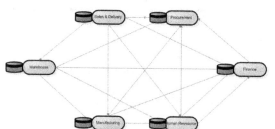

decentralised architecture with many stand-alone applications per department with no integration between them, which meant a lot of non-synchronised master data.

1. Anarchical IT architecture

SAP keeps on evolving for 40 years now:

- They keep on developing a strong branding over the years that positions them as the leading management software for large size companies (more than 50% of the market);
- They maintain a global growth by expanding on different industries, that is the reason why today they have more than 25 vertical industry solutions[4], and that they try to win new markets with static and preconfigured solutions;
- They keep on expanding the scope of their solution via new developments, acquisitions[5] or stakes in specialised companies. These companies are either leaders on the software development side or consulting companies with in-depth competencies in a given industry sector.

2. Centralised & Integrated architecture

Year	Acquisitions	Stakes	Divestitures
2011	2	1	1
2010	1	1	1
2009	3	0	1
2008	6	2	2
2007	5	0	0
2006	5	4	0
2005	5	0	1
2004	2	1	1
2003	2	0	0
2002	3	0	3
2001	4	2	1
2000	0	2	1
1999	3	4	1
1998	0	5	1
1997	0	1	0
1996	0	2	1
1995	0	0	0
1994	0	1	0
1993	0	2	1
1992	0	0	0
1991	0	0	0
1990	0	0	1
Total	41	28	17

3. SAP Acquisition table

---

[4] see section "Part II: The client's solution evaluation – Features Coverage - Verticals: Industry Solutions
[5] The latest well known acquisitions are:
- OutlookSoft, so as to replace the old SAP consolidation module;
- Sybase, so as to develop small local databases on smartphone platforms.

As SAP, the ERP foundation and market evolve.

If we look at the ERP foundation evolution, we can identify three major periods.

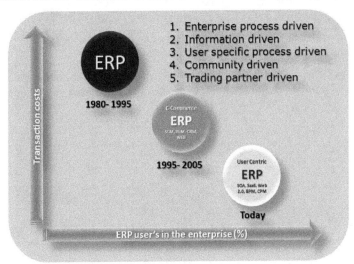

1. Enterprise process driven
2. Information driven
3. User specific process driven
4. Community driven
5. Trading partner driven

4 .ERP evolution

The <u>first period</u> represents the globalisation of the ERP, very expensive in comparaison with the total number of transactions and the small number of users. The <u>second period</u> takes into account the internet opportunities on a process driven approach with a constant increasing number of users. We are now in the <u>third period</u>, with a user centric approach supported by the current technologies such as SOA, Web 2.0, etc.

If we look at the ERP market evolution, the interest for <u>large size companies</u> to have their business supported by an information system has been for years a well known key success factor. But today, it is also a key success factor for the <u>small and middle size companies</u>. Like any large size company, they have to achieve the same main goals:

- Being <u>more profitable</u> in conformity with legal regulations;
- Keeping on <u>developing their core processes</u> in order to stay at the forefront;
- <u>Outsourcing</u> parts of their business worldwide (production, sales, etc...);
- Remaining at the leading edge of the <u>latest technologies</u>;
- <u>Dealing with different actors</u> in a heterogeneous IT landscape;

- <u>Being productive and reactive</u> in a constant evolving world in terms of economy, technology and geographical expansion; and last but not least
- <u>Reaching the objectives</u> fixed by the company's strategy.

With the globalisation of the business, every company now needs to be supported by an agile and consolidated system offering fast and clear results at low cost.

In this evolving world, the open source software is an alternative to the proprietary software more adapted to specific entities of large size companies and to SMEs.

Part I

OpenERP's Solution Maturity

1. Overview

We make the assumption that for a number of clients the ERP solution must mainly sustain the functionalities of the "support processes" whereas the functionalities of the specific "core processes" are handled by dedicated applications.

When buying an ERP system, the clients will consider 6 different criteria in order to evaluate the existing ERPs on the market: the Market Position, the Features & Business Coverage, the Technical Quality, the Customisation & Flexibility, the Productivity-Ergonomy & Ease of Use, and finally the Total Cost of Ownership (TCO).

Market Position

Strength of the channel, available offline and online marketing material, existence of brochures, a strong brand, press success stories, etc.

Features & Business Coverage

Do you have the features I need? Based on a list of requirements, a client usually wants to select a software covering most of his needs or providing a solution that fits a specific industry such as Retail, Health, Associations, Public Sector, etc.

Technical Quality

How does the solution support the development of specific requirements? How does the technical quality impact the TCO and the flexibility of the product?

Customisation & Flexibility

Ability of software to easily adapt to different users and system requirements: integrated workflow, designing reports, etc.

Productivity, Ergonomy & Ease of Use

This is a new client's requirement that has appeared a few years ago with the user centric approach, iPad apps, cloud applications, etc. Today, the client needs applications that are out-of-the-box and easy to use.

Total Cost of Ownership (TCO)

The Total Cost of Ownership is critical for any client in today's market. They cannot risk unwise investments with recurrent costs without concrete results.

The "Blue Ocean Wave" graph below is the consolidated result of the client's 6 concerns that are presented in more detail in the next chapters.

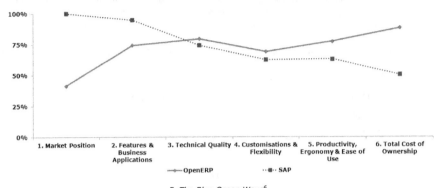

5. The Blue Ocean Wave[6]

This figure clearly describes the maturity and the strategy of both companies.

For each criterion analysed, the depth and breadth is estimated with a tolerance margin. We use the gauge to display the results. The gauge plots the estimated weighted scores of all functionalities for each criterion along a separate axis that goes from the centre to the outer ring of the chart; the outer ring representing the client expected solution. The values used in the graphics are based on the information collected near 4200 users via the web site: http://www.evaluation-matrix.com/. Based on our own experience, we have re-evaluated some aberrant values (see annex). To be pragmatic, we will only detail the most relevant functionalities compared with the selection criteria identified by the clients. For some criteria, the ERPs can cover more than the client's expectations but the focus is kept on the solution expected by the client, consequently representing a scope of 100%.

---

[6] Blue Ocean Marketing Strategy: A slang term for the uncontested market space for an unknown industry or innovation. Coined by professors W. Chan Kim and Renee Mauborgne in their book "Blue Ocean Strategy: How to Create Uncontested Market Space and the Make Competition Irrelevant" (2005), blue oceans are associated with high potential profits.
Read more: http://www.investopedia.com/terms/b/blue_ocean.asp#ixzz1cjkbMaJJ

2. Market Position

The market position has a strong impact on the trust the client has when buying the solution. It indicates how the product, the brand and the vendor are perceived by the market.

The market position criterion can be defined into 4 sub-criteria:

- **Visibility**: the hit number on Google search engine;
- **Service offer**: the number of integrators/partners;
- **Success stories**: the number of success stories;
- **Software vendor strength**: the number of employees.

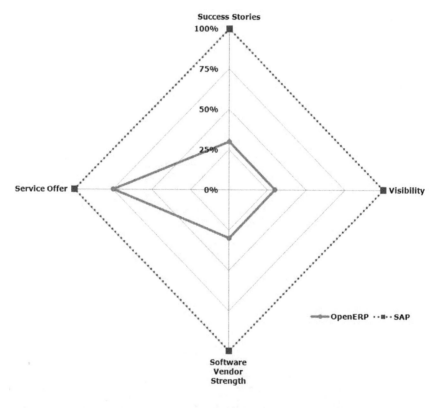

6. Market position gauge

2.1.Visibility

The visibility analyses the *brand market recognition*. For that, we will refer to the "Google Trends"[7] tool, the number of books written, of Twitter followers and the estimated number of events organised by the software vendors.

	SAP	OpenERP (qty)	OpenERP vs SAP (%)
Hits on Google	233M[8]	1,49M	0,6%
Books on Amazon.com	8800	13	0,15%
Followers on Twitter	13516	2793	20%
Official Events / Months	70[9]	39	55%

7. SAP vs OpenERP - Brand analysis, in October 2011

Google Trends counts the searches performed by visitors on the internet worldwide since 2004. In the relative mode, the data is scaled to the average search traffic for your term (represented as 1.0) during the time period you've selected.

Searches on the SAP keyword are stable but have slightly decreased (20%) since 2008, as shown in the graph below.

[7] http://www.google.be/trends
[8] M: for Million Hit
[9] http://www.sap.com/events/event-results.epx

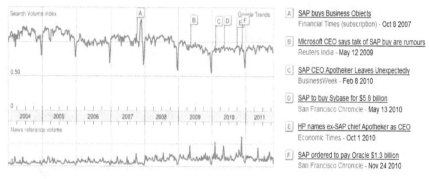

A	SAP buys Business Objects Financial Times (subscription) - Oct 8 2007
B	Microsoft CEO says talk of SAP buy are rumours Reuters India - May 12 2009
C	SAP CEO Apotheker Leaves Unexpectedly BusinessWeek - Feb 8 2010
D	SAP to buy Sybase for $5.8 billion San Francisco Chronicle - May 13 2010
E	HP names ex-SAP chief Apotheker as CEO Economic Times - Oct 1 2010
F	SAP ordered to pay Oracle $1.3 billion San Francisco Chronicle - Nov 24 2010

8. Google Trends: searches on the "SAP" keyword

The name OpenERP appeared for the first time in 2008 and its visibility has grown very quickly since then.

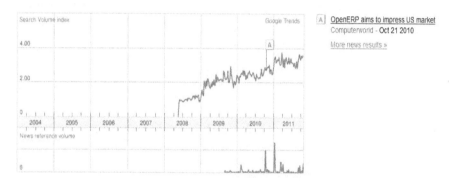

A	OpenERP aims to impress US market Computerworld - Oct 21 2010 More news results »

9. Google Trends: searches on the "OpenERP" keyword - Fast growth

But OpenERP was first labelled under the name of TinyERP which was launched in 2005. As the software grew very quickly, it was renamed OpenERP for marketing reasons in 2008. In order to analyse the trend of the brand over this period of time, we have taken both keywords: TinyERP & OpenERP.

openerp ━━━ 1.00   tinyerp ━━ 0.36

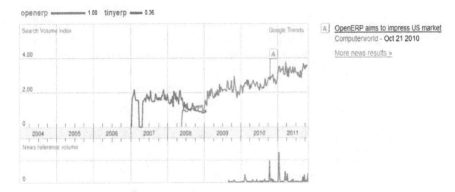

A] OpenERP aims to impress US market
Computerworld - Oct 21 2010

More news results »

10. Google Trends: searches on the "TinyERP"+"OpenERP" keywords

SAP still has a strong advance in terms of brand recognition. As shown in the picture below, **SAP** still generates around 260 times more search requests than OpenERP.

openerp ·1.00   tinyerp ·0   sap ━━━ 268

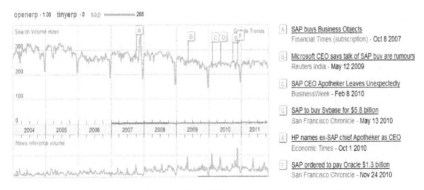

A] SAP buys Business Objects
Financial Times (subscription) - Oct 8 2007

B] Microsoft CEO says talk of SAP buy are rumours
Reuters India - May 12 2009

C] SAP CEO Apotheker Leaves Unexpectedly
BusinessWeek - Feb 8 2010

D] SAP to buy Sybase for $5.8 billion
San Francisco Chronicle - May 13 2010

E] HP names ex-SAP chief Apotheker as CEO
Economic Times - Oct 1 2010

F] SAP ordered to pay Oracle $1.3 billion
San Francisco Chronicle - Nov 24 2010

11. Google Trends: SAP has 268x more searches than OpenERP

2.2.Service offer

Both SAP and OpenERP follow a global strategy in order to develop their software. They both have a good internationalisation of the accounting that allows them to be border independent. The map below shows all the countries where SAP is.

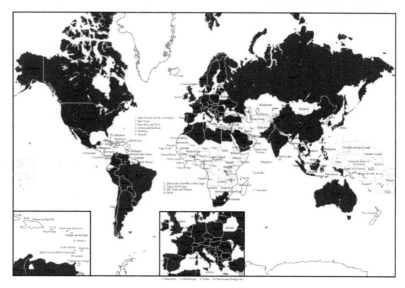

12. Countries where SAP has a presence

OpenERP's partner network is quite young and mostly composed of small to medium size IT companies. OpenERP has around 500 partners in 78 countries[10].

The map below shows all the countries where OpenERP has official partners which have been trained and certified and which provide implementation services.

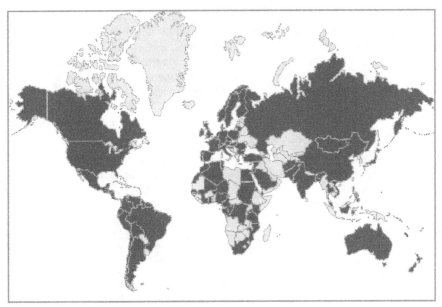

13. The OpenERP Partner Network

OpenERP SA, the OpenERP software vendor, is a medium size company with around 200 employees in 4 offices worldwide. They are located in Belgium (Brussels & Grand-Rosière), United-States (California), and India (Ahmadabad).

---

[10] 300 partners in 78 countries : Value provided by the software vendor in November 2011

Looking at the Market position gauge, it is clear that the market maturity of OpenERP is far from the one of SAP.

OpenERP's strategy is to invest the minimum in marketing and to focus rather on the product development. They do not publish a lot of books on their product. They limit their marketing activities to:

1. **Leverage the communities:** the OpenERP communities are many and very active. They concern partners, users and contributors but there are also social communities like Facebook[11], Twitter[12], LinkedIn[13] as well as development communities like launchpad, OpenERP's official forum, etc;

2. **Educate through events:** OpenERP organizes a lot of international events (online and on site) to promote the software. These events are taking place worldwide and are usually organized jointly between a partner and OpenERP SA.

OpenERP's solution homepage is a good example on how they leverage the communities to communicate on OpenERP instead of doing it directly. When you log on to OpenERP, you will see a page allowing you to select the application you want to use. On the right side, OpenERP integrates a feedback of its users in real time (this feature can be deactivated from your homepage).

14. OpenERP Tweets area

[11] http://www.facebook.com/OpenERP
[12] http://twitter.com/#!/OpenERP
[13] Go to OpenERP LinkedIn Group

The market position of the two software vendors is different by the key messages used in their communication, as summarised in the table below:

SAP		OpenERP
Promote the company (SAP vs SAP R3)	→	Promote the product: OpenERP
Buyer and sponsors: CFO, COO	→	Buyer and sponsors: IT Guys
We can do everything!	→	We do what you need!
Publish studies, comparisons, awards	→	Leverage communication through the users
Good, strong success stories	→	Thousands of references
Remain the leader	→	Be the most widely used
Mature Software	→	Agile Software
Brand growth mainly supported by the marketing department	→	Brand growth only supported by the communities

It is clear for us that OpenERP must quickly change its client's approach from the IT buyer to the business buyer and increase the number of success stories with exhaustive references on the scope covered.

3. Features Coverage & Business Applications

The Features Coverage & Business Applications criterion concerns two main dimensions: the Business Application Coverage and the Industry Solutions.

3.1.Business applications coverage

The analysis refers to the most common business applications.

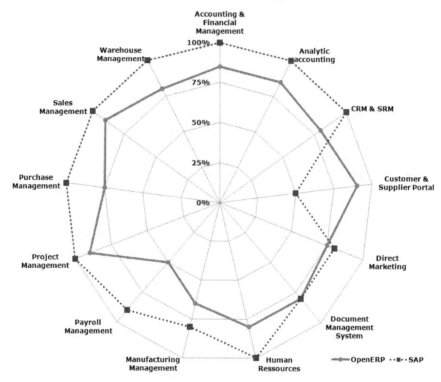

15. Business Applications gauge

It is obvious that SAP is more advanced than OpenERP in most analysed business applications and that for several of them SAP meets entirely the clients' standard requirements. This result is no surprise: OpenERP is younger on the market and it is just a question of time before it offers more.

Indeed, OpenERP profits from three accelerators:

1. <u>OpenERP is an open source application</u>. This means the possibility of a free redistribution of new developments, access to the source code and to the derived works and solutions.
2. An open source application also means that the product is <u>developed by a community</u>. Today, the community gathers more than 2 500 developers besides the 200 developers employed by the software vendor. Community is not synonymous with anarchy. The software vendor acts as an <u>orchestra leader</u> in the community. He guides the development and approves the quality and the legitimacy of what has been developed.
3. The OpenERP architecture and <u>platform allow very fast developments</u> (Agile method). Indeed, developing the same functionality in SAP requires at least three times more resource time spent than in OpenERP (see chapter "Technical Quality).

This table shows the number of modules developed from the beginning of OpenERP up to 2011. Currently, 1 745 modules have been developed (December 2011). As described above and showed in the diagram below, the number of module increases exponentially.
According to this model, there will be 6 000 modules by 2016 ...

janv-05	40	
janv-06	50	
janv-07	112	
janv-08	195	OpenERP SA
janv-09	350	
janv-10	750	
janv-11	1.250	
janv-12	1.905	
janv-13	2.683	
janv-14	3.583	Extrapolation
janv-15	4.606	
janv-16	5.751	

It is important to point out that the concept of module in OpenERP does not correspond with the one of SAP. A SAP module covers a functional scope that can be compared to a department of a company (e.g. Sales-*SD*, Procurement-*MM*, Accounting-*FI*, etc.). In the context of OpenERP, a module gathers a restricted set of specific functionalities (Charts of Accounts-*account_chart*, Accounting Stock Management-*account_stock*, Account For Multicompany- *account_multicompany*, etc.).

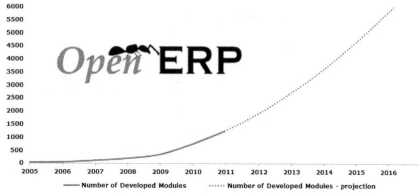

16. Evolution of developed modules

Looking at the development figures, we observe that they follow an exponential curve. OpenERP is catching up on its functional coverage. The main functionalities required by the community[14] today and under development concern:

- Advanced treasury management (cash flow statement, accounting budget, etc.);
- Budgetary management for the Public Sector i.e. Fund Management;
- Simplification of the multi-company customisation (in progress);
- Improvement of the financial reporting for the local administration;
- Native integration with Jasper reporting soft (in progress);
- MRP II;
- Quality Control Management;
- Supplier ranking;
- Payroll engine & country specific pre-configuration payroll (in progress).

In terms of business applications, we can see some other great features integrated in OpenERP such as:

- Fully-integrated Geographical Information System (GIS) added at the core level using PostGIS;
- Web interface extended with OpenLayers;
- High-capability of integration with other tools;
- Etc.

---

[14] http://feedback.openerp.com/forums/

24

3.1.1. Fully-integrated Graphical Information System (GIS)

At the beginning of 2011, OpenERP and Camptocamp have decided to merge their know-how and explore a new environment which included both an ERP and a GIS system (GeoEngine), leading the way to a cutting edge technological adventure, in perfect alignment with the open source spirit. Camptocamp[15] is one of the first OpenERP Gold Partners (2004) and also a leading European actor (software vendor and integrator) in the open source GIS.

The integration of Camptocamp's GIS is a nice example of the flexibility and speed of integration of OpenERP's framework with a new solution. It only took two months between the decision to integrate the tools and the POC implementation. This rapidity is due to the approach of the open source itself which makes it possible for the solution developer to re-use existing libraries enabling to integrate instead of interfacing.

The OpenERP v6.1 will have the entire GIS tool integrated into the OpenERP Database Server, allowing the interaction between the table views and the map in order to:

- Display the location of partners or any other geo-referenced information;
- Generate thematic maps based on the selected/combined/aggregated information from the end user's interaction with the traditional table view of OpenERP.

Integrated into the core of the tool, this coming version of OpenERP will then be the first ERP to provide such functionality (watch the demo screen cast[16])! Until now, the ERP had to be interfaced with the GIS solution, which required replication and synchronization of data into several databases. Here, GeoEngine is a tool based on OpenObject but it can work independently from OpenERP as well.

By adding this new dimension to the core of OpenERP, many new business applications will become effortless. It will be possible to display marketing data on a map with sales revenue per city, per country, etc. or directly on the address of the client; or even to show the asset list of a room directly on the building map. There are multiple applications possible such as:

- Geographical queries and filters (e.g. list of the last sales made within 10km of a point of sale);
- Geo-marketing (e.g. client areas analysis, direct marketing);
- Logistics optimization (e.g. stock location);
- Assets localization;

---

[15] www.camptocam.com
[16] Demo GIS on OpenERP screen cast: http://bit.ly/dWTVAB

- Improvement of distribution flows (e.g. find shorter way to deliver customers);
- Fleet management (vehicles, boats, etc.);
- Dashboards;
- Crisis management;
- Etc.

It is also possible to create and personalize maps directly from the user interface.

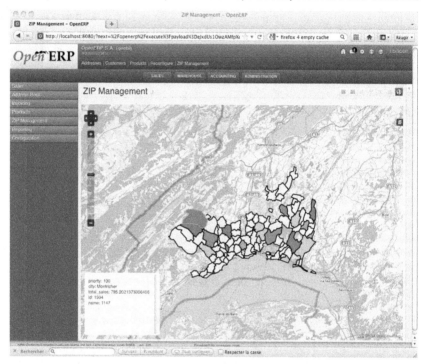

17. Sales Revenue per ZIP code

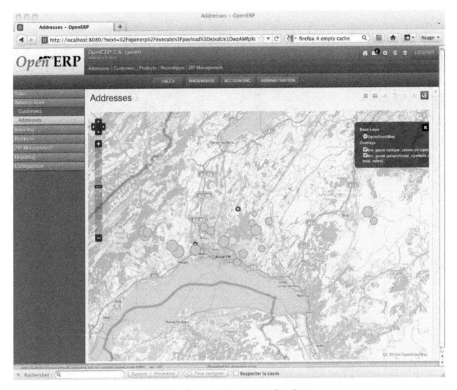

18. Sales Revenue per customer location

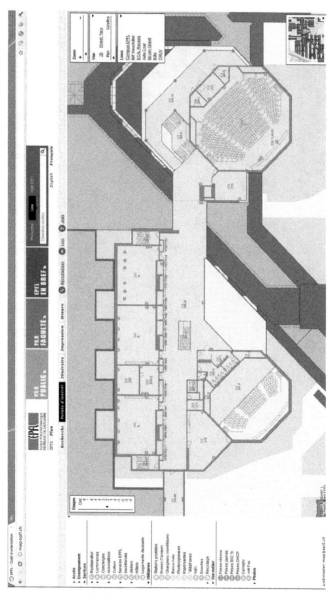

19. Asset positioning into a building

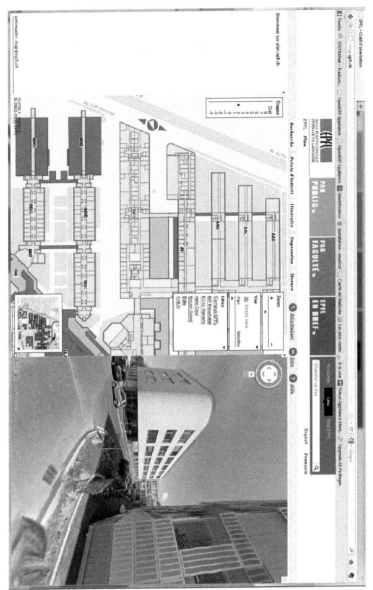

20. Google street map into building map

Camptocamp OpenERP GeoEngine overview

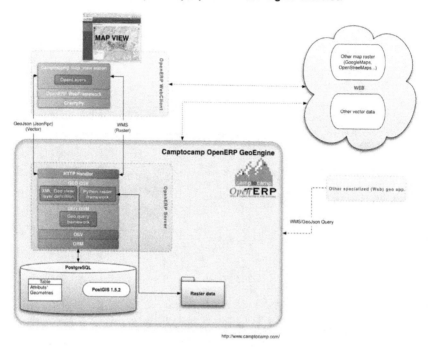

21. Camptocamp's GIS & OpenERP Server integrated architecture

3.1.2. High capability of integration with other tools

OpenERP is an open source software also open to other software by means of a middleware and a dedicated plug-in. For example: Magento, Spree, OS Commerce, OOOR connector, Kettle ETL/BI, Asterik, etc. but also SAP (by using API & IDOC)!

One of the most interesting projects of integration with SAP is the Danone project.

"*Although Danone is a significant SAP client, the industry giant decided to use an open source integrated ERP solution for the emerging countries where it operates. OpenERP was identified as a good SAP alternative for Danone small entities. OpenERP was integrated in three entities of Danone in Columbia, Argentina and Australia. Although the company has invested a lot for several years implementing SAP, it proved not to fit the needs that Danone had in the green field entities. From 2007, the structure of the group has changed, finding itself in the position to manage smaller entities that were not necessarily generating big revenue. So, implementing their core model in SAP didn't make sense. Consequently, a less expensive and more flexible solution was sought, allowing faster implementations. Even though SAP covers a large array of needs, it's non-modular integrated software, leaving not much room for errors. Currently, Danone develops a platform in order to synchronise OpenERP with SAP*"[17].

Other connectors exist also with Thunderbird, Outlook, etc.

---

17 http://www.01net.com/editorial/542324/danone-deploie-ses-progiciels-integres-avec-agilite-et-succes/

3.2.Industry solution (Verticals)

Concerning the second dimension of the Features Coverage & Business Applications criterion (i.e. the different industry solutions proposed), SAP offers more than 25 industry-specific solutions which provide a pre-customised system adapted to the standard process used in the selected industry.

In order to develop one industry solution, SAP's development team creates an industry map defining the standard processes in collaboration with industry-specific user groups and partners.

SAP currently offers the following industry sets:

22. SAP's vertical applications

OpenERP satisfies the specific needs of the industry in another way. As OpenERP has been developed on a modular structure, assembling the modules differently allows it to answer the industry's specific needs.

OpenERP's modules cover a lot of industries such as:

- Association Management;
- Health / Hospitals / Medical;
- Manufacturing Industries;
- Services;
- Retail;
- Auction Houses;
- Logistics;
- Point-of-Sales;
- Food industries;
- Etc.

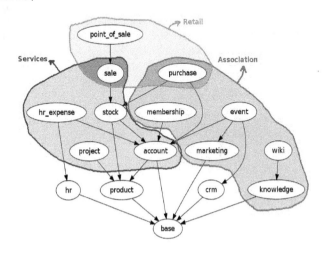

23.Group of modules as industry solution

Most of these vertical applications are developed and promoted by OpenERP's partners having business experience in these specific areas.

4. Customisation & Flexibility

The software flexibility is its ability to easily change according to different users and system requirements: designing processes, reports, screens, etc.

This criterion is critical when selecting an ERP system since midmarket companies, like any others, need an agile system adaptable to a fast moving business environment.

On top of being flexible, the system has to be easily configurable. This often helps to reduce the budget of the implementation project and the system maintenance. Customizing usually represents a significant part of the ERP project, as explained in the following chapter.

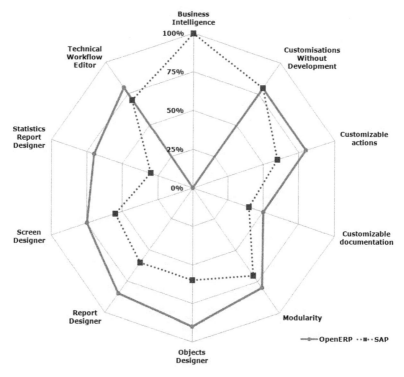

24. Customisation & Flexibility gauge

The Customisation & Flexibility gauge shows that both solutions are flexible even though there are significant differences between them.

The **Screen Designer** tool in OpenERP requires no development. A user or a functional consultant, for example, can easily hide, add or remove a field. It only takes a few seconds. In SAP we would rather use any "unused" field so as to avoid developments requiring specific competencies and to guarantee an easy version upgrade afterwards.

In OpenERP, the **Technical Workflow Editor** in which the validation steps of a process are designed is an easy visual tool (see Figure 27: Purchase order workflow). No specific competences are required except for complex workflow rules where a Python[18] developer will support the consultant.

Concerning the **Report Designer** tool, SAP provides static reports on the transactional data by default but most of their clients use Business Object for advanced reports. In OpenERP, standard reports exist in most transactions including: drill-down, drill-up, drill-across, switch to graph view, custom filters, import/export in different formats, different graphic representations, etc.

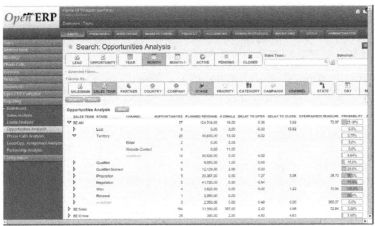

25. *Sales Pipeline Analysis in OpenERP Opportunities of the month, grouped by sales teams, stage and channel*

---

[18] Python (Definition from WIKIPEDIA) is a general-purpose, high-level programming language whose design philosophy emphasizes code readability. Python claims to "[combine] remarkable power with very clear syntax", and its standard library is large and comprehensive. Its use of indentation for block delimiters is unique among popular programming languages. Python supports multiple programming paradigms, primarily but not limited to object-oriented, imperative and, to a lesser extent, functional programming styles. It features a fully dynamic type system and automatic memory management, similar to that of Scheme, Ruby, Perl, and Tcl. Like other dynamic languages, Python is often used as a scripting language, but is also used in a wide range of non-scripting contexts. Using third-party tools, Python code can be packaged into standalone executable programs. Python interpreters are available for many operating systems.

In addition to these standard reports, OpenERP report designer makes it possible to extend reports or create new ones. In this case, it's necessary to work with developers for specifics reports or functionalities not yet developed in the existing modules.

For **Business Intelligence** (BI), SAP provides a complete BI suite with a data warehouse, an ETL with SAP connectors (Extraction, Transformation, Loading) and reporting tools such as Business Object, BeX, etc. OpenERP does not have a BI native tool, but it supports traditional BI software connection since PostgreSQL is ODBC full compatible. If the client needs to consolidate information from different databases or software, the installation of Business Object or an open source alternative like Pentaho or JasperReport is required.

Concerning the **Modularity**, meaning the possibility to reuse and distribute existing configuration as well as to define or easily reorganize menu, OpenERP and SAP use a different approach. In each application, SAP provides nearly all possible features by default. The configuration goes through configuring all the features, setting all parameters. The fineness of the module granularity in OpenERP enables to only install what the client needs. As the application is lighter, the configuration becomes lighter too. You can quickly configure without developing any new module. When the client requests something which is not in OpenERP or in SAP, a development must be budgeted. We will develop this specific subject in the "Technical Quality" chapter.

The **Configuration/Customisation** works differently for each solution. In SAP, the configuration of the standard processes is made through a dedicated centralised transaction (SPRO) in which a number of business rules are defined. The copy-control rule for instance allows to copy data from a reference document type to a subsequent document type.

In OpenERP, the configuration can be made in two different ways. The first one is through a configuration menu decentralised at each business application level. The second one is through the combination of master data values and its workflow engine in which dynamic objects are associated (sales orders, purchases, timesheets, etc.). The workflow nodes are actions to be executed on the object. OpenERP allows different kind of actions:

- Methods to be executed on the object, generally developed in a module;
- Actions to be configured from the user interface such as sending an email, creating/updating an object, launching a report, etc.

The workflow arrows define the condition to be checked to go to the next node. These can either be a condition on the object (sale.invoice.paid==True), on the user interface (the user has to click on a button to validate an invoice) or on the security (the user must be sales manager to validate the order). For example, in the purchase order workflow shown below, a draft invoice and/or goods receipt are/is created at saving time according to the values filled in some specific fields.

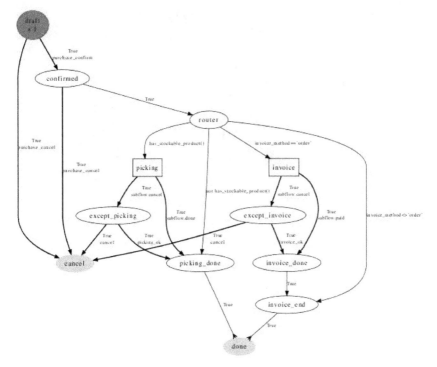

26. Purchase order workflow

When implementing an out-of-the-box solution (only configuration), the configuration effort required to fit OpenERP to the client's needs is reasonable thanks to its different native tools (screen designer, report designer, etc).

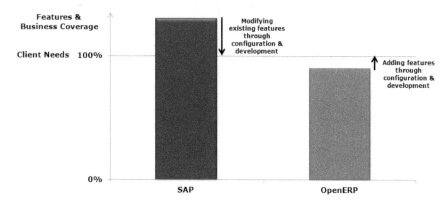

27. OpenERP and SAP way of handling the client's needs

5. Total Cost of Ownership (TCO)

The "Total Cost of Ownership" [19], usually abbreviated as TCO, is a calculation designed to help people to take financial decisions with full knowledge of the facts. Rather than just looking at the purchase price of an object, the TCO looks at the complete cost from purchase to disposal. It adds to the initial purchase price other costs incurred during the life of the product, such as service, repair, and insurance.

The TCO is heavily used in the IT industry. When they evaluate the purchase of a computer or a system, they usually take into account the purchase, repairs, maintenance, upgrades, service and support, networking, security, training, and software licenses as well. The costs included in a TCO evaluation can get as complex as the concept map[20] displayed below.

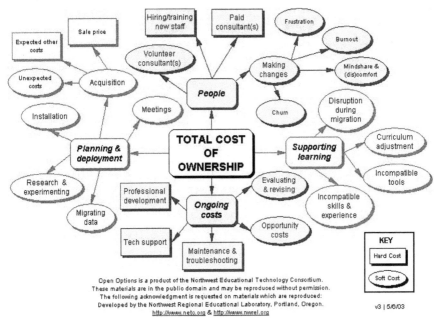

28. Total Cost of Ownership Model

---

[19] **Total Cost of Ownership (TCO):** http://management.about.com/od/money/a/TCO.htm
[20] http://management.about.com/od/money/a/TCO.htm

Our ERP costing model[21], part of a complex TCO, includes the consulting and software vendor costs. The client's internal resources cost and the costs generated by the client's IT department are not considered here. We have assessed this model based on a case study which is a solution with standard processes (FI/CO - SD - MM - CRM) for a middle market company (500 to 999 users) with only 15% specific requirements. Over a 5 years period, we plan one major software upgrade including data migration (for instance, SAP3.1 to 4.0, SAP 4.6 to ECC or OpenERP 5.14 to 6.01. We take here into account three main cost groups:

- **Implementations cost**:
  - **Project management**, with Project Support Office (PSO costs) and Project Management Office (PMO costs);
  - **Customisation**, regrouping the activities of analysis, configuration and development;
  - **Change management**, regrouping training and coaching activities.
- **Installation cost**:
  - **License**;
  - **Hardware** including the **Integration cost** of the system in the IT landscape of the company (OS installation, Firewall, Backup, ERP Installation, etc.)
- **Maintenance cost**, including upgrade and support costs.

We also consider that there is a strict project governance. The project scope is clearly defined and accepted by the client and the consulting teams. A project manager is assigned at the client side. This project manager is able to manage the client's team (key users, steering committee) and he is acknowledged and empowered to take decisions.

---

21 Figures are presented in annex.

5.1.The implementation cost

In a SAP project, the **project management** cost represents 10% of the implementation cost. It is generally admitted that it can reach 25% when the project manager has no real decision power and that there is no project support officers (PSO) appointed. The **customisation** cost represents around 60% of the implementation cost. And a global envelop of 30% is allocated for all the **change management** aspects, with 60% of this envelop allocated to training and the rest to coaching/reorganization.

The implementation cost of an OpenERP project is also composed of 10% for the **project management,** 60% for the **customisation** and 30% for the **change management**. But compared to SAP, this implementation cost (same scope, same number of users) is reduced by 30% to 40% thanks to the customisation. Indeed, OpenERP architecture and technology allow to perform quickly and easily a number of activities such as:

- Creating reports;
- Workflow adaptation;
- New process creation;
- Uploading batch files for data migration;
- Adding fields;
- Customizing screens;
- Defining interface;
- Implementing authorisations;
- Configuring.

As a conservative approach for the costing model built below, we consider a 30% reduction of the implementation cost. This percentage is based on our experience and feedback from OpenERP's partners.

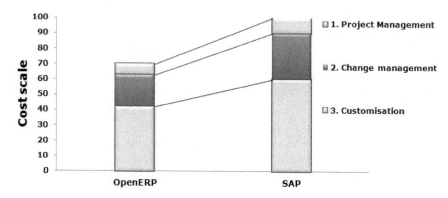

29. Implementation cost by stream

Looking at the implementation cost in detail, we observe that all sub-costs are reduced in the same way.

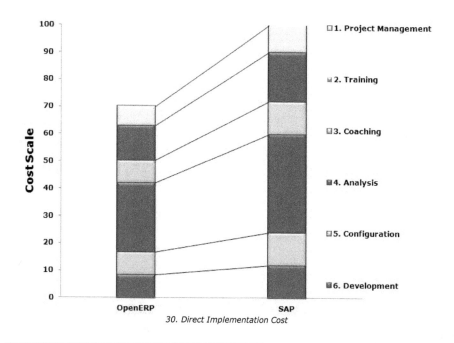

30. Direct Implementation Cost

5.2.The installation cost

In a SAP project, it is usually considered that the global **license cost** represents 25% more than the implementation cost. In other words, the implementation costs 4 times more than the global license package. This is a usual ratio, not a rule. It is also admitted that the **hardware cost** represents around 10 % of the implementation cost. This cost takes into account not only the hardware aspect but also the **integration cost** with the company's IT landscape, the backup tools and the server configuration, the firewall, the documentation, the governance, the internal training and finally the SAP installation on the different servers.

In our case study, the SAP IT landscape will look like this, using dedicated servers for CRM.

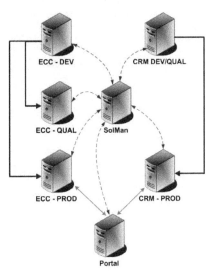

31. SAP Landscape

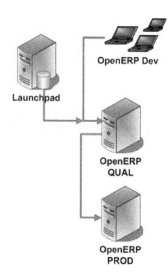

OpenERP Dev

Launchpad

OpenERP
QUAL

OpenERP
PROD

With OpenERP, the IT landscape will rather be different. It is drastically reduced thanks to its technical approach based on the middleware technology. For security and performance reasons, it is recommended to have two physical environments even though there is a real separation between the instances on a same machine. Notice that no dedicated servers are used for CRM because it is integrated into OpenERP.

The installation cost of OpenERP is cut down because there is **no license cost** and the **hardware** requirements are limited.

32. OpenERP Landscape

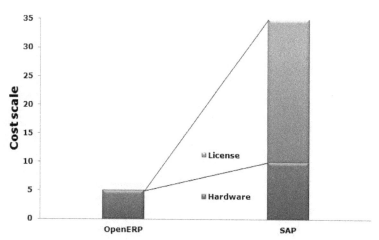

33. Installation cost

5.3. The maintenance cost

In a SAP project, the **maintenance cost** represents an annual budget allocated for a period of five years in order to maintain, support and upgrade the system. The official yearly SAP maintenance fees represent 24% of the global license cost. In other words, it represents 6% of the implementation cost . With its **maintenance contract**, SAP regularly delivers patches and bug fixes. But in case of a major release, as foreseen in our case study, the client needs to launch a new project with external consultancy services. This additional upgrade cost must be supported by the client. Pay attention to the notice published on the 13th of October 2011 where SAP announces that *"SAP users should plan for a migration of their NetWeaver-based applications to SAP's HANA Architecture within the next three to five years. At the same time, users must determine if there are opportunities to improve their Advanced Business Application Programming (ABAP) applications with the new infrastructure"*[22]. This reinforces the idea that the client must even plan an upgrade budget every 3 or 4 years.

OpenERP calculates its **maintenance cost** in another way. Up to 150 users, it is a fixed amount according to the number of users (from 1..10, 10..25, 25..70, 70..150). Above 150 users, it is a negotiated price with the software vendor. The OpenERP's **maintenance contract** covers the patches, bug fixes and the upgrades (conversion/migration script) for the standard and certified modules. In our case study, as there are between 500 and 999 users, the software vendor estimates the annual maintenance fees to 10% of the estimated implementation cost.

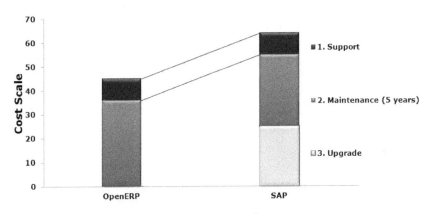

34. Cost Maintenance over 5 years

[22] SAP Throws Down the Next-Generation Architecture Gauntlet With HANA

5.4.The ERP costing model

The model over a 5 years period shows that with a conservative approach, the implementation & utilization costs decrease from a coefficient of 214 for SAP to 135 for OpenERP. During the 1st implementation year, this coefficient goes from 160 for SAP to 100 for OpenERP. Concretely, for the same scope with standard functionalities (+15% specific requirements) and with the same consulting scale rate, we can estimate that the ERP budget is reduced with OpenERP by around 40% during the first year as well as over the period of 5 years.

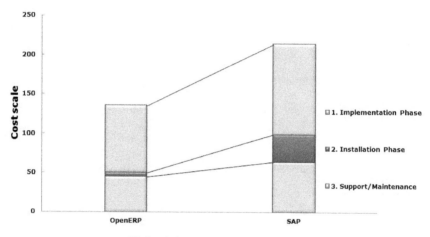

35. Cumulative costs over 5 years by solution

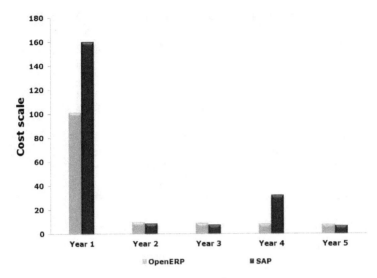

36. Annual costs over 5 years

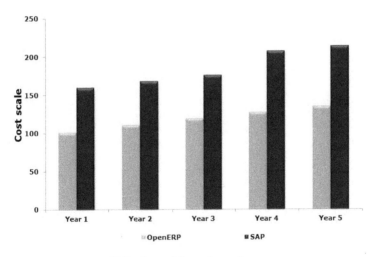

37. Yearly cumulative costs over 5 years

6. Technical Quality

The technical quality criterion shows how the solution easily supports the development of specific requirements (non-standards functionalities). It indicates as well how the solution architecture adheres to the sound principles of the current IT standards.

The axes analysed to score the technical quality are:

- **Efficiency**: the source code and software architecture attributes are the elements that ensure the high performance of a system;
- **Accessibility**: many interface accesses to the server (GTK, web, etc.);
- **Database flexibility:** number of databases supported;
- **Debugger**: ability to debug from the client or server, ability to trace a full process;
- **Modularity**: ability to package creation, modification as module, code units separately defined;
- **Security:** ability to define the authorisation access level.

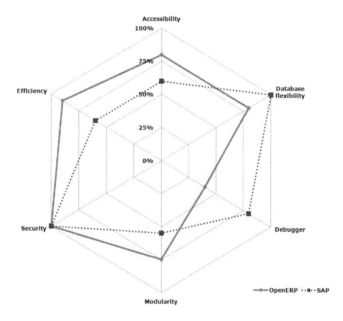

38. Technical Quality gauge

6.1.Efficiency

We consider here three elements of high interests: the **architecture**, the **database** and the **programming language**.

6.1.1. Architecture efficiency

OpenERP has been developed using a service-oriented architecture, meaning that every object defined in the application is automatically exposed to the activated web-services. These web-services are complete: they allow to perform any kind of operation. They are used by the OpenERP clients (the web client or the rich GTK client) to access the different components of the application. This means that the whole business logic and security layer are implemented on the server side, not on the client side. Moreover, an encrypted web-service is used to access the OpenERP server from another computer whereas a non-encrypted web-service is used when both the client and the server are installed on the same computer.

The web-services provided by the OpenERP server are:

- XML-RPC: a standard protocol oriented on method calls, over HTTP;
- XML-RPC over HTTPS: an encrypted HTTPS;
- NETRPC: which is specific to OpenERP but faster than XML-RPC.

The OpenERP server contains all the components of a powerful application development framework:

- Object database (ORM);
- Workflow engine;
- Several reports engine;
- Several web-services interface;
- Translation engine;
- Module system;
- Integrated test platform;
- MVC architecture[23].

---

[23] http://en.wikipedia.org/wiki/Model%E2%80%93view%E2%80%93controller

The Model–view–controller (MVC) is a software architecture currently considered as an architectural pattern used in software engineering. The pattern isolates "domain logic" (the application logic for the user) from the user interface (input and presentation), permitting independent developments, testing and maintenance independent from each other (separation of concerns). Model View Controller (MVC) pattern creates applications that separate the different aspects of the application (input logic, business logic, and UI logic), while providing a loose coupling between these elements.

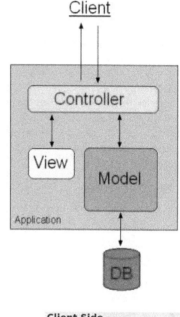

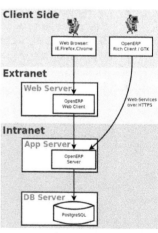

The main components of an OpenERP installation are:

- Database: PostgreSQL;
- OpenERP Server, containing:
  - Application framework;
  - Modules implementing the business features;
- OpenERP Client, providing the user interface with:
  - Web Client to use with your browser without any installation;
  - Rich Client that should be installed on the user computer.

39. Communication layers

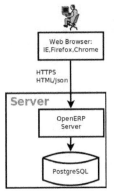

Depending on the needs of the client, the web client can be installed as a module of the OpenERP server, so that only two components are to be installed to run a fully working OpenERP: the OpenERP server and the database, both running on the same physical server. So, the minimal IT infrastructure looks like this.

All the features of the OpenERP server are accessible from the Rich or the Web client interfaces.

40. Server layers

Concerning SAP, it has evolved from ABAP architecture to a service-oriented architecture with its current SAP Netweaver platform.

SAP NetWeaver[24] is SAP's integrated technology computing platform and is the technical foundation for many SAP applications since the SAP Business Suite. SAP NetWeaver is marketed as a service-oriented application and integration platform. SAP NetWeaver provides the development and runtime environment for SAP applications and can be used for custom development and integration with other applications and systems. SAP NetWeaver is built using primarily the ABAP programming language, but also uses C (programming language), C++, and Java EE. It also employs open standards and industry de facto standards. It can be extended with technologies such as Microsoft .NET, Java EE, and IBM WebSphere with which it interoperates.

SAP NetWeaver release is considered as a strategic move by SAP for driving enterprises to run their business on a single integrated platform that includes both the applications and the technology. Industry analysts refer to this type of integrated platform offer as an "appli-structure" (applications + infrastructure). According to SAP, this approach is driven by industry's needs to lower IT costs through an enterprise architecture that is at once:

- More flexible;
- Better integrated with applications;
- Built on open standards to ensure future interoperability and broad integration; and
- Provided by a vendor that is financially viable in the long term.

---

[24] http://en.wikipedia.org/wiki/SAP_NetWeaver

SAP is fostering relationships with system integrators and independent software vendors, many of the latter becoming "Powered by SAP NetWeaver".

SAP NetWeaver is part of SAP's transition plan to a more open, service-oriented architecture and to deliver the technical foundation of its applications on a single, integrated platform and common release cycle.

NetWeaver is essentially the integrated stack of SAP technology products. The SAP Web Application Server (sometimes referred to as WebAS) is the runtime environment for the SAP applications—all of the mySAP Business Suite solutions (SRM, CRM, SCM, PLM, ERP) run on SAP WebAS.

As seen in the chapter "Total Cost of Ownership", the architecture needed for an OpenERP installation is lighter than the one needed for a SAP installation.

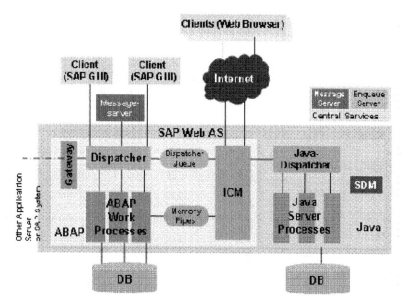

41. Components of the Web Application Server

6.1.2. Database efficiency

PostgreSQL, the database of OpenERP is very similar in terms of features and performance to Oracle or SAP databases. Both are relational databases, compliant with the SQL language, so that one developer will easily move from one to another.

Instead of directly using SQL queries, **OpenERP has an Object-Relational Mapping**[25] technology on top of the database that allows to directly manipulate objects instead of the database queries. As an example, the instantiation of the following object:

```
class book(osv.osv):
 _name = "book"
 _columns = {
        'title': fields.char('Book Title', size=64, required=True),
        'author': fields.many2one('author', 'Author')
        }
```

It will automatically create the related table in the PostgreSQL database:

```
CREATE TABLE book (
 id INT PRIMARY KEY,
 title VARCHAR(64) NOT NULL,
 author INTEGER REFERENCES partner,
)
```

There are a lot of advantages to use an object relational mapping instead of making direct SQL queries to access the data. As an example, have a look at the following code:

```
book = self.browse(cr, uid, id=5)
country_name = book.author.address.country.name
```

---

[25] **Object-relational Mapping** (ORM, O/RM, and O/R mapping) in computer software is a programming technique for converting data between incompatible type systems in object-oriented programming languages. This creates, in effect, a "virtual object database" that can be used from within the programming language. There are both free and commercial packages available that perform object-relational mapping, although some programmers opt to create their own ORM tools. From http://en.wikipedia.org/wiki/Object-Relational Mapping

It will be converted to the following queries in SQL:

```
cr.execute("SELECT author FROM book WHERE id=%d", (5,))
author_id = cr.fetchone()[0]
cr.execute("SELECT address FROM authors WHERE id=%d", (author_id,))
address_id = cr.fetchone()[0]
cr.execute("SELECT   country   FROM   address   WHERE   id=%d",
(address_id,))
country_id = cr.fetchone()[0]
cr.execute("SELECT name FROM country WHERE id=%d", (country_id,))
country_name = cr.fetchone()[0]
```

The Object-Relational Mapping engine also allows smart optimisation of the queries generated to fasten the OpenERP accesses to the database. Being able to efficiently optimize the query performed on the database is important as the database is the bottleneck of the performance of all ERP systems.

Let's say that for example, you want to make a report of your sales by product category. The category of product is a field on the product object. The product is stored on the sale order line, and the sale order line is linked to the sale order. If you want to analyse 100 sales orders you will use the following code in OpenERP:

```
result = {}
sales = self.browse(cr, uid, ids)
for sale in sales:
        for line in sale.lines:
                result.setdefault(line.product.category, 0.0)
                result[line.product.category] += line.price
```

Due to the optimization, prefetching and caching of the OpenERP ORM engine, the above code will only generate 3 queries. Even if you read 100 sales orders having each 5 links, it only performs one query per table.

The same code without an ORM, with direct queries performed on the database, would look like this:

```
result = {}
for id in ids:
    cr.execute("SELECT id,product_id,price FROM sale_order_line
    WHERE order_id=%s", id)
    for (line_id, product_id, price) in cr.fetchall():
        cr.execute("SELECT category FROM product WHERE
        id=%d", (product_id,))
        category = cr.fetchone()[0]
        result.setdefault(category, 0.0)
        result[category] += price
```

6.1.3. Programming language efficiency

Concerning the programming language, SAP uses ABAP4[26] whereas OpenERP uses Python.

The code below performs the same action in SAP/ABAP and in OpenERP/Python. It is a report[27] that lists the users of the system in a specific order, displaying the following fields: user-id, client, printer, profiles.

Note that the normal way to develop a report in OpenERP is not the one presented here. The Python code below follows the ABAP code so as to be able to compare the code lines necessary to perform a same action.

Usually, reports in OpenERP are created as objects linked to a PostgreSQL view and an XML view, allowing the report to be fully customizable in the web interface (filters, drill down, groups, etc). And the result, in terms of development effort, is nearly the same (around 15 lines of code).

A report in SAP/ABAP	The same report in OpenERP/Python

REPORT ZSBEN002 LINE-SIZE 120 LINE-COUNT 90.
-- 	
* Description: The report creates a user list. *
* Parameters: Mand, when ' ': sort by user
*
*   when 'X': sort by client   *
	def user_list_get(self, cr, uid, sort='name'):
	
	  # Description: print a list of users
	  # Parameters: sort: the column used to sort
	  # Output: list of users and their data

---

[26] **ABAP** (Advanced Business Application Programming, originally *Allgemeiner Berichts-Aufbereitungs-Prozessor*, German for "general report creation processor"), is a high-level programming language created by the German software company SAP. It is currently positioned, alongside the more recently introduced Java, as the language for programming the SAP Application Server, part of its NetWeaver platform for building business applications. The syntax of ABAP is somewhat similar to COBOL. ABAP is one of the many application-specific fourth-generation languages (4GLs) first developed in the 1980s. It was originally the report language for SAP R/2, a platform that enabled large corporations to build mainframe business applications for materials management and financial and management accounting.
ABAP used to be an abbreviation of *Allgemeiner **B**erichtsaufbereitungsprozessor*, the German meaning of "generic report preparation processor" , but was later renamed to **A**dvanced **B**usiness **A**pplication **P**rogramming. ABAP was one of the first languages to include the concept of *Logical Databases* (LDBs), which provides a high level of abstraction from the basic database level(s).
The ABAP programming language was originally used by developers to develop the SAP R/3 platform. It was also intended to be used by SAP customers to enhance SAP applications – customers can develop custom reports and interfaces with ABAP programming. The language is fairly easy to learn for programmers but it is not a tool for direct use by non-programmers. Knowledge of relational database design and preferably also of object-oriented concepts is necessary to create ABAP programs.
ABAP remains the language for creating programs for the client-server R/3 system, which SAP first released in 1992. As computer hardware evolved through the 1990s, more and more of SAP's applications and systems were written in ABAP. By 2001, all but the most basic functions were written in ABAP. In 1999, SAP released an object-oriented extension to ABAP called ABAP Objects, along with R/3 release 4.6.
SAP's current development platform NetWeaver supports both ABAP and Java.
[27] From http://www.guidancetech.com/people/holland/sap/abap/

```
* Authorisation: S_USER_GRP, User Master
Anzeigen *
* Class:        Report              *
* R/3 Release:  3.0d                     *
* Programmer:   Bence Toth            *
*-------------------------------------------------*
TABLES: USR04, USR01, TSP03.
PARAMETERS: MAND.
DATA: BEGIN OF U4 OCCURS 0,
      MANDT LIKE USR04-MANDT,
      BNAME LIKE USR04-BNAME,
      MODDA LIKE USR04-MODDA,
      MODTI LIKE USR04-MODTI,
      MODBE LIKE USR04-MODBE,
      NRPRO LIKE USR04-NRPRO,
      PROFS LIKE USR04-PROFS.
DATA: END OF U4.
DATA: X TYPE I VALUE 2.
DATA: Y TYPE I VALUE 1.
DATA: Z TYPE I.
FIELD-SYMBOLS: <A>.

TOP-OF-PAGE.
  ULINE (102).
  WRITE: / '|Name','        |Cli.
|','Prin.|','Mod.date  |',
         'Creator       |','User Profile', 102 '|'.
  ULINE (102).
  SKIP.
  ULINE (102).

END-OF-SELECTION.

  AUTHORITY-CHECK OBJECT 'S_USER_GRP'
        ID 'CLASS' FIELD '*'
        ID 'ACTVT' FIELD '03'.
  IF SY-SUBRC NE 0. EXIT. ENDIF.

  REFRESH U4.
  CLEAR U4.
  SELECT * FROM USR04 CLIENT SPECIFIED.
    MOVE-CORRESPONDING USR04 TO U4.
    APPEND U4.
    CLEAR U4.
  ENDSELECT.
  IF MAND EQ ' '.
    SORT U4 BY BNAME MANDT.
  ELSE.
    SORT U4 BY MANDT BNAME.
  ENDIF.
  LOOP AT U4.
* Check that all profiles of the user is on the
same page   Z = ( SY-LINCT - SY-LINNO ) - (
```

```
# Security is handled automatically
# according to the current user




result = ['Name', 'Company',
'Mod.date',\
          'Creator', 'Lang']




    ids = self.search(cr, uid, [],
_order=sort)
    for user in self.browse(cr, uid, ids,
c=c):


        result.append([
          user.name,
user.company_id.name,
          user.write_date,
user.create_uid.login
          user.context_lang
        ])
```

```
U4-NRPRO - 2 ) / 36 - 1.
  IF Z LE 0. NEW-PAGE. ENDIF.
  FORMAT INTENSIFIED OFF.
  SELECT SINGLE * FROM USR01 CLIENT
SPECIFIED WHERE
                     MANDT EQ U4-MANDT
AND
                     BNAME EQ U4-BNAME.
  SELECT SINGLE * FROM TSP03 WHERE
PADEST EQ USR01-SPLD.
  WRITE: / '|',U4-BNAME INTENSIFIED ON,
       '|',U4-MANDT,
       '|',USR01-SPLD,
       '|',U4-MODDA,
       '|',U4-MODBE,'|'.
  ASSIGN 1 TO <A>.
  DO.
   ASSIGN U4-PROFS+X(12) TO <A>.
   IF <A> EQ '        '.
    EXIT.
   ENDIF.
   Y = ( X - 2 ) / 12.
   IF Y NE 0.
    Y = Y MOD 3.
    IF Y EQ 0.
  WRITE: / '|         |    |    |       |
|'.
    ENDIF.
   ENDIF.
   WRITE: <A>,'|'.
   ADD 12 TO X.
  ENDDO.
  WHILE X > 38.
   X = X - 36.
  ENDWHILE.

  CASE X.
   WHEN 26.
    WRITE: '        |'.
   WHEN 38.
   WHEN 14.
    WRITE: '        |         |'.
   WHEN 2.
    WRITE: '        |         |         |'.
   WHEN OTHERS.
    WRITE: / 'ez az:', X.
  ENDCASE.
  X = 2.
  Y = 1.
  WRITE: / '|         |----------------------------
----------------
--------------------------------------|'.
   AT END OF BNAME.
```

```
print '-' * 90
for line in result:
  print
'|%20s|%15s|%9s|%10s|%9s|' % line
```

```
   POSITION 1. WRITE '---------------'.
   ENDAT.
* New-page at the end of each Client, when
sorted by client
   AT END  OF MANDT.
     CHECK MAND EQ 'X'.
     NEW-PAGE.
   ENDAT.
  ENDLOOP.
```

Comparison of SAP/ABAP code (left) and OpenERP/Python code (right) making the same report.

Making the same report requires 111 lines of **ABAP** in **SAP** whereas only 13 lines of Python are necessary in OpenERP.

With this example, we easily catch the main advantage of the Python language. Python is a high level and efficient language, very easy to read and to learn.

For instance, the ORM enables to browse through all the data we need with one single line of code, and by default the security is managed according to the connected user (uid).

6.2.Security

The SAP authorisation[28] concept protects transactions, programs, and services in SAP systems from unauthorized access. The administrator assigns authorisations to the users that determine which actions a user can execute in the SAP System, after he has logged on to the system and authenticated himself.

In order to access business objects or to execute SAP transactions, a user requires corresponding authorisations, as business objects or transactions are protected by authorisation objects. The authorisations represent instances of generic authorisation objects and are defined depending on the activity and responsibilities of the user. The authorisations are combined in an authorisation profile that is associated with a role. The user administrators then assign the corresponding roles using the user master record, so that the user can use the appropriate transactions for his tasks.

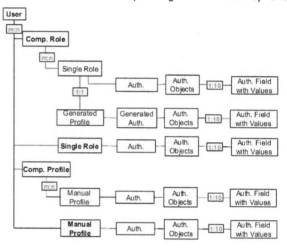

42. SAP authorisation components and their relationships

OpenERP provides several security mechanisms, all implemented at the lowest level of the server, which is the ORM engine. Security rules are attached to groups (Sales Manager, Accountant, etc) and a user can be assigned to several groups.

By default, a user has no access right. The more we assign groups to the user, the more he gets rights to perform some actions. A group can inherit all the rights from another group.

You can also define rules that are global, so they are applied to all users indiscriminately of the groups they belong to. For example, the multi-company

---

[28] http://help.sap.com/saphelp_nw04/helpdata/en/52/671285439b11d1896f0000e8322d00/content.htm

rules are global (a user can only see invoices of the companies he belongs to). Like SAP, OpenERP is pre-configured with best-practices.

You can assign several security rules at the group level, each rule being of one type: access rights, record rules, record fields and workflow transitions.

OpenERP "Access Rights" are rules that define the access a user can have on a particular object: sale order, invoice, client, etc. An access right can give the authorisation to read, write, create or delete the object. By default, it gives access to all records of the object.

When accessing an object, records are filtered based on record rules. A record rule is a condition that each record must satisfy to be read, written, created or deleted. An example of rule on a business opportunity can be: salesman = connected_user. It means that the connected user can only see opportunities in which he is flagged as the salesman.

Every field of an OpenERP object can be access-controlled (record fields). For example, you can say that the margin field on a sale order is accessible by sales manager only.

Finally, the workflow transitions determine the right to go from one step to another in the workflow, for example, from a draft to a validated invoice.

6.3.Other technical quality aspects

Concerning the **accessibility**, there are several user interfaces for OpenERP. Since its 6.0 version, the main user interface is a web client accessing the OpenERP server through web-services. It is also a web server accessible from any browser: Internet Explorer (>=7), Firefox, Google Chrome or Safari (Mac, iPad).

But some other user interfaces are optionally provided:

- Mobile interface: to access through your mobile phone (see EEZEE-IT[29]);
- Official GTK rich client: to install on the user computer;
- Unofficial KDE rich client: that has been provided by the community.

Regarding the **database flexibility**, the positioning of OpenERP is lower because OpenERP exclusively uses PostgreSQL Database, an open source database able to support the equivalent workload of Oracle.

Unlike SAP, we could be surprised by the lack of a **native debugger**, but the community provides many powerful debugging tools. An example among others: KOMODO IDE[30], but also Eclipse, PyDev, Visual Studio, and even 3D debuggers.

---

[29] http://www.eezee-it.com/openerp-mobile.html
[30] http://www.youtube.com/watch?v=CtjX3QYopuo and http://www.activestate.com/komodo-ide

7. Productivity, Ergonomy & Ease of Use

This criterion is one of the main focuses of OpenERP's research and development centre. We will analyse it through five sub-criteria:

- **Information Accessibility**: public resources and communities with forums, information repository, books reference, availability of source code and extra features;
- **Ease of use**: learning curve speed, documentation accessibility and availability, ease of installation;
- **Ergonomy**: the rich or the web Graphical User Interface, type of views such as Gantt or Kanban, native Dashboarding, Data analysis (filtering, searching, etc.);
- **Information visibility**: the type of information displayed;
- **Productivity**: fast encoding entries, presentation of data into the screens, integration with external software as Microsoft Office, OpenOffice, mail client, webmail.

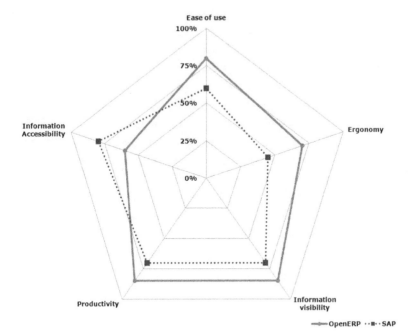

43. Productivity, Ergonomy & Ease of Use

7.1.Information visibility

The type of view is defined at the user level: extended or simplified. The extended view displays all the information for the transaction whereas simplified view restricts the display to specific information.

Take the example of a product displayed with the rich client.

With a simplified view

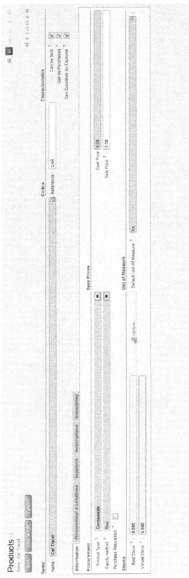

44. OpenERP simplified view

With an extended view

Products :
Name: Car Travel

Name:
Name: Car Travel
Variants:

Tabs: Information | Procurement & Locations | Suppliers | Descriptions | Packaging | Accounting

Procurement

Product Type ? : Consumable
Procurement Method ? : Make to Stock
Supply method ? : Buy
Purchase Requisition ? :

Weights

Volume ? : 0.000
Gross weight ? : 0.000
Net weight ? : 0.000

Stocks

Real Stock ? : 0.000
Virtual Stock ? : 0.000

Unit of Measure

Default Unit Of Measure ? : km
Purchase Unit of Measure ? : km

Codes

Reference : CAR
EAN13 :

Base Prices

Costing Method ? : Standard Price
Cost Price ? : 0.00
Sale Price ? : 0.39
Variant Price Margin : 1.00
Variant Price Extra : 0.00

Status

Category ? : All products / Private
Status ? :
Product Manager ? :

Lots

Track Manufacturing Lots ? :
Track Incoming Lots ? :
Track Outgoing Lots ? :

Second UoM

Unit of Sale ? :
UOM -> UOS Coeff ? : 1.0000
Measure Type : Fixed

Characteristics

Can be Sold ? :
Can be Purchased ? :
Can Constitute an Expense ? :

Update

45. OpenERP extended view

7.2.Ergonomy

In both user interfaces (Web or GTK), documents can be displayed from several different views depending on user's need. There are six main OpenERP views, illustrated in the screenshot below:

1. The calendar view to schedule meetings, tasks, deliveries, manufacturing orders, etc.

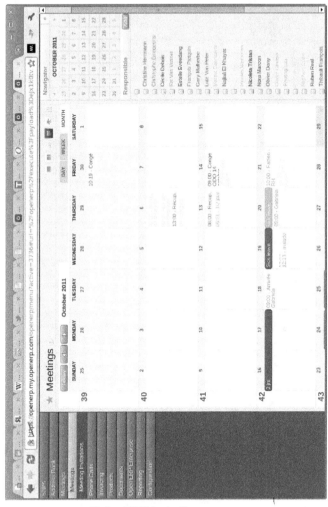

46. OpenERP Calendar View

2. The Gantt chart view to schedule tasks, work orders, etc.

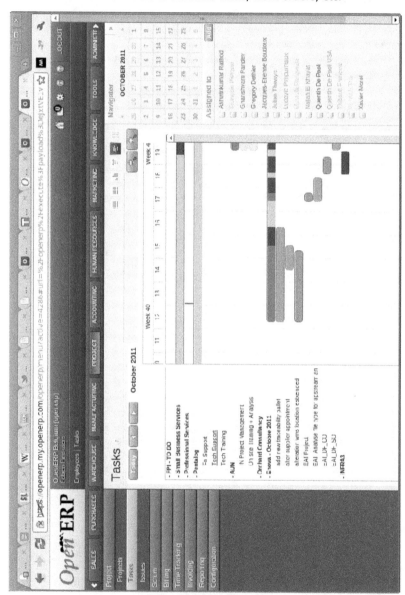

47. OpenERP Gantt chart view

3. The dashboard view with a graph

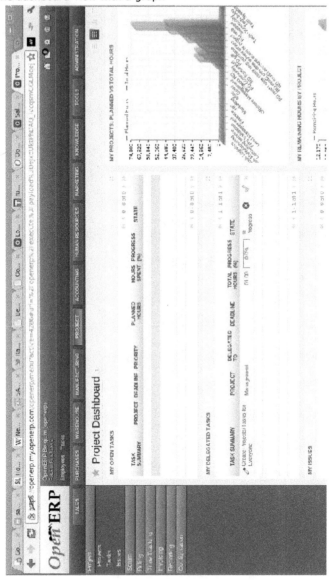

48. OpenERP Dashboard view

4. A search and list view: opportunities pipeline analysis grouped by sales team and salesman

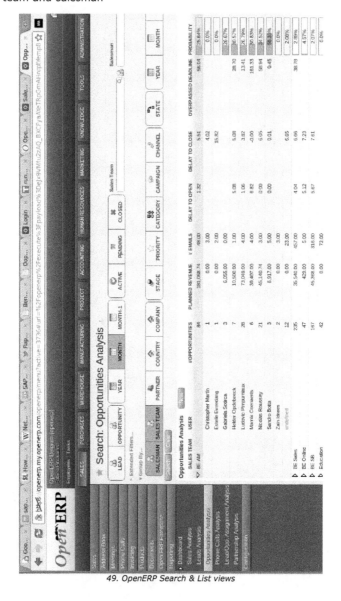

49. OpenERP Search & List views

5. The Kanban view to manage tasks in the process, CRM opportunities, brain storming, etc

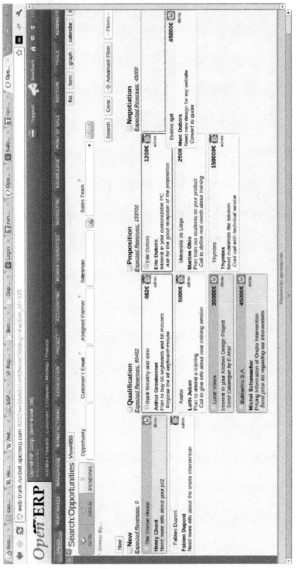

50. OpenERP Kanban view

6. The process view showing the status of any document in the process

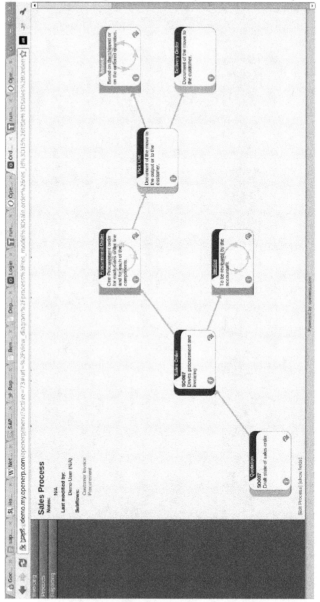

51. OpenERP Process view

7.3.Productivity

7.3.1. The Akretion case.

The Akretion Company tested the OpenERP user interface resulting in a productivity benchmark[31]. They hosted an OpenERP server in a datacentre and they asked some users to perform two business flows as quickly as possible. The scenario consisted of a full purchase workflow (request for quotation, purchase order, reception of goods, and control of the supplier invoice) and a full sale workflow (quotation, delivery order, client invoice). The users manually executed this scenario several times, on different versions of OpenERP. They kept the fastest timing measured.

On the OpenERP web interface, they performed the two flows (covering 7 different documents) in 1 minute en 40 seconds. Note that on a local installation (without the network latent period) the time to perform these two flows is 25 seconds.

7.3.2. The Kanban view

In the new 6.1 version, OpenERP has developed a Kanban view, a visual process view that tells what to produce, when to produce it, and how much to produce. The objective is to increase the productivity of an OpenERP user via a dedicated interface.

The four properties required for a successful Kanban implementation are covered by OpenERP Kanban view[32]:

- **Visualize the workflow**

    Today, the knowledge of the workflow is inherently not visible as it is "hidden" in the information systems. Visualizing the flow of work is essential to understand how work runs. Making the right changes without this understanding is harder. Usually, workflows are visualized using a card wall with cards and columns: the columns representing the different stages of the workflow and the cards the feature/story/task/result of it. OpenERP has replaced the card wall by the Kanban view interface.

---

[31] http://www.akretion.com/en/blog/2011/10/27/benchmarks-with-openerp-server-hosted-on-the-internet/
[32] Kanban View will be in version 6.1 planned for January 2012

- **Limit Work In Progress (WIP)**

  Limiting work-in-progress implies that a pull system is implemented on all or part of the workflow. The pull system will act as one of the main stimuli to make continuous, incremental and progressive changes to your system. As work is pulled from the preceding stage, it is critical to limit it to the capacity available within the local WIP.

- **Manage Flow**

  The flow of work at each stage of the workflow must be monitored, measured and reported.

- **Improve Collaboratively** (using models & the scientific method)

  The Kanban method encourages small continuous, incremental and progressive changes. When teams have a shared understanding of theories about work, workflow, process and risk, they are more likely able to build a shared comprehension of a problem and to suggest improvement actions agreed by consensus.

7.3.3. A business scenario

Now let's compare productivity with a same **business scenario** running in both applications.

Note that for the OpenERP case, screenshots are based on the web interface.

The business scenario[33] is the following:

> A customer has placed an order with company ABC Computers Inc. for 10 computers to be delivered on the 10th of March. The customer typically pays with Net30, but this time for this order, he wants a Net 60 payment term.

---

[33] This scenario has been found on SAPLab: http://saplab.org/2011/02/how-to-create-a-sales-order-in-sap-part-1/

Creating a sale order in SAP

Step No. 1: Use the Transaction Code [VA01] to create the Sales Order in SAP. Alternatively, you can use the menu path as shown in the picture below [Logistics -> Sales and Distribution -> Sales -> Order -> Create]

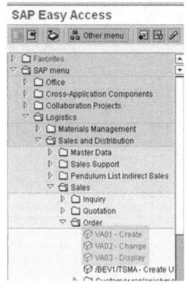

52. SAP Sales transaction code

Step No. 2: Use the document type "OR" in the Order Type field.

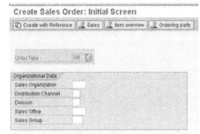

53. SAP Sales document type selection

Select a Customer (let's say customer number: 1400) and enter some text in the Customer PO Number field and either hit the return key or the Green check mark button. This will ensure that SAP will validate the data you have entered.

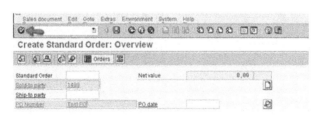

54. SAP sold to party (customer) selection

Step No. 3: Enter a material number and quantity. We have chosen a material of M-01 (representing Computer product) and a quantity of 10 based on the scenario. The corresponding material descriptions and other information are automatically pulled up by SAP.

Standard Order			Net value		850,00	EUR
Sold-to party	1400	A.I.T. GmbH / Landsbergerstrasse 54 / D-50997 Koeln-Rondorf				
Ship-to party	1400	A.I.T. GmbH / Landsbergerstrasse 54 / D-50997 Koeln-Rondorf				
PO Number	Test PO		PO date			

Sales | Item overview | Item detail | Ordering party | Procurement | Shipping | Reason for rejection

Req. deliv.date	D	28.02.2011	Deliver.Plant			
Contract start			Contract end			
☐ Complete dlv.			Total Weight		168	KG
Delivery block			Volume		1,500	M3
Billing block			Pricing date	21.02.2011		
Payment card			Exp.date			
Card Verif. Value			Incoterms	CFR	Köln	
Payment terms	ZB01	14 Days 3%, 30/2%, ·				

All items

Item	Material	Order Quantity	Un	Description	S	Customer Material Numb
10	M-01	10	PC	Sunny Sunny 01	☐	TEST
					☐	
					☐	

55. SAP sales item entry

Step No. 4: As you can see in the above picture, SAP automatically proposed a Requested Delivery date (28/02/2011). This data is retrieved from the lead time configuration in the Sales Order. However, since the customer has requested that the goods to be delivered on March 10th, let's change the requested delivery date.

Hint: Always change the Requested Delivery Date before entering the line items.

Sales | Item overview | Item detail | Ordering party | Procurement | Shipping | Reas

Req. deliv.date	D	14.03.2011	Deliver.Plant			
Contract start			Contract end			
☐ Complete dlv.			Total Weight		168	KG
Delivery block			Volume		1,500	M3

56. SAP Sales requested delivery date entry

Step No. 5: Since the customer has requested a change in the Payment terms, let's select the right payment term from the SAP Search Help.

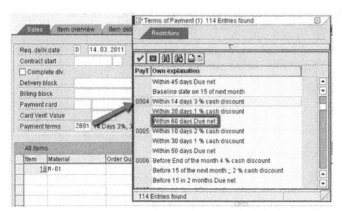

Since the customer has requested a payment term of NET 60, we are selecting a payment term of '0004' – Within 60 days due net.

57. SAP Sales terms of payment selection

Step No. 6: Once you are done with the Sales Order creation, click on the save button. SAP will display the order number at the bottom.

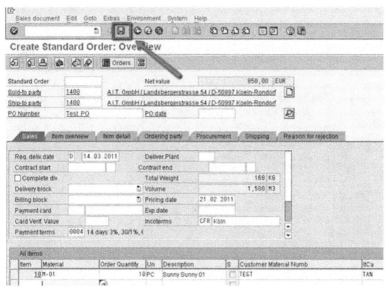

58. SAP save the sales document

Standard Order 13216 has been saved

Creating a sale order in OpenERP

Step No. 1: Use the menu [Sales / Sales Orders] to view, edit and create the Sales Order in OpenERP.

Note that in OpenERP, the same menu and screen are used to create, view or modify documents.

59. OpenERP Menu

Step No. 2: From the list of sales orders, click on the [New] button to create a new sale.

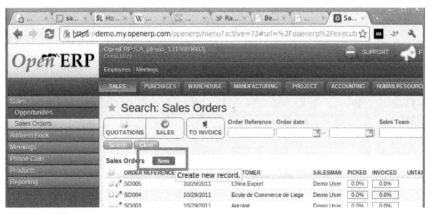

60. Creating a new sales order in OpenERP

Step No. 3: From the customer field, select your customer. You can write the name of the customer or his code. As you type in the name, OpenERP proposes you in real time the customers with similar names for a quick search (self completion functionality).

After selecting the customer, all the other fields are automatically pulled up by OpenERP: the delivery and invoicing addresses, the pricelist, the delivery methods, etc.

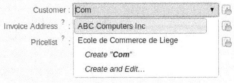

61.Selecting a customer in OpenERP

62. Creating a new sales order line in OpenERP

In order to facilitate the users' life, documents in OpenERP look like their paper version. So, the sale order form looks like the real one with header, sale order lines and footer with the untaxed amount, the taxes and the total.

In order to achieve this, OpenERP only shows the limited number of fields usually used according to the module installed. Data of less importance are put in other tabs.

Step No. 4: Click on the "New" icon on the right of the "Sale Order Lines" section to create a new line with a product and a quantity. Select your product in the same way that you have selected your customer.

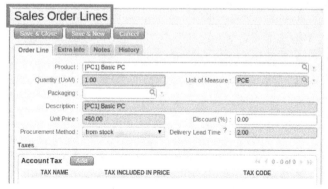

63. Selecting the material in OpenERP

Step No. 5: From the "Other Information" tab, you can change the default payment term of the customer and select the "30 Days End of Month" payment term.

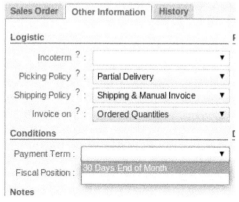

64. Selecting the term of payment in OpenERP

Step No. 6: Once you have created your Sale Order, you can save and confirm it by clicking on the "Confirm Order" button at the bottom right corner.

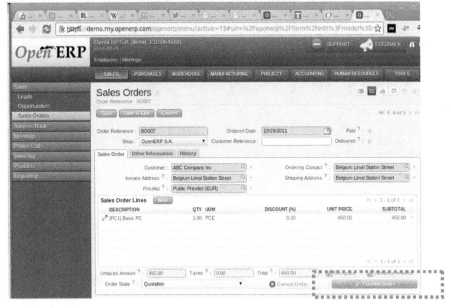

65. Confirming & Saving the sales order in OpenERP

OpenERP will display the log of every document created and operation scheduled. You can click on any of the line to zoom to that document.

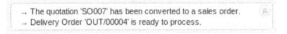

→ The quotation 'SO007' has been converted to a sales order.
→ Delivery Order 'OUT/00004' is ready to process.

8. Conclusion

After having identified, scored and balanced the selection criteria of an ERP, we have gathered them together. We can visualize through the "Blue Ocean Wave" diagram the strengths and weaknesses of the two solutions in relation to client's expectations, which are 100%.

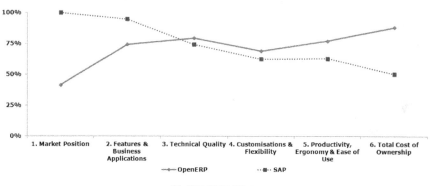

66. Blue Ocean Wave

To end our analysis, we will position the two products according to two dimensions: the strategy of the software vendor and the performance of the solution. This positioning is displayed in the **«Alignment quadrant»**.

The strategic dimension of the software vendor represents its vision in terms of marketing (Market Position), development of functionalities (Features Coverage & Business Applications) and technical platform (Technical Quality).

The performance dimension of the solution for a client is linked to the ease of configuration (Customisation & Flexibility), the acceptance rate (Productivity, Ergonomy & Ease of Use) by the users and the cost of acquisition and installation (TCO).

As each criterion does not weigh in the same way in the client's decision, it is necessary to apply a weighting before gathering them together in one of the two dimensions. We have defined three type of weighting: High (0.8), Standard (0.5) and Low (0.2).

The Market position of a supplier compared to another is important; nevertheless it has a **standard** rating because within the context of SMEs, there is an open-mindedness to innovation.

The Features Coverage & Business Applications represents a priority for SMEs' leaders. This functional coverage guaranties a quality and rapidity of implementation as well as an ease to update the solution. The client is looking for a solution that answers his needs. This criterion has a **high** rating.

Despite the ERP is considered as "Business Critical", the current technologies used to support the ERP are efficient, secure, etc. It is for that raison that the "Technical Quality" criterion has a **standard** rating in the client's perception.

The implementation of an ERP creates lots of fears amongst the prospective buyers. The decision makers fear to embark on a journey with no near end. The clients tend to forget that it is the complexity they want to implement in the ERP which is a brake to the good achievement of the project. All requirements identified are not always covered by the solution. In that case, specific developments will have to be made. The ease to implement them and to parameterize the solution (Customisation & Flexibility) are taken into account by the decision makers; giving a **high** rating to this criterion.

Even if the ergonomy and the ease of use seem to be significant criteria of acceptance, SMEs don't give them priority. The functionalities must first meet the needs of the client. The Productivity, Ergonomy & Ease of use criterion has a **standard** rating.

SMEs are very sensitive to the market moods, and they cannot risk an unwise investment with recurrent costs. The TCO is thus essential in the decision making process and for this reason it has a **high** rating.

		Score by criterion		Weighted score by criterion		
		OpenERP	SAP	Weighting	OpenERP	SAP
Enterprise Strategy	1. Market Position	42%	100%	0,5	12%	28%
	2. Features & Business Applications	74%	95%	0,8	33%	42%
	3. Technical Quality	80%	74%	0,5	22%	21%
				1,8	67%	91%
Product Performance	4. Customisations & Flexibility	69%	63%	0,8	26%	24%
	5. Productivity, Ergonomy & Ease of Use	77%	63%	0,5	18%	15%
	6. Total Cost of Ownership	88%	50%	0,8	34%	19%
				2,1	78%	58%

67. The table summarizes the weighted rating of the criteria presented in the "Blue Ocean Wave" diagram.

		Weighted Score by Dimension	
		OpenERP	SAP
Dimension	Enterprise Strategy	67%	91%
	Product Performance	78%	58%

68. Strategy & Performance Alignment

Alignment Quadrant

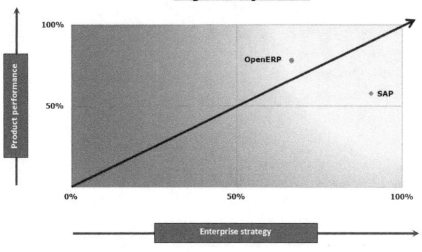

69. This quadrant clearly resumes the maturity and the strategy of both companies

The positioning of the two solutions with their software vendor shows their strengths and weaknesses. The product performance of SAP is significantly below the strategy developed. Although today SAP product is more powerful than the one of OpenERP, the latter is more in adequacy with its strategy and it even exceeds it.

It is clear that the future of SAP and OpenERP will be settled in the short run. If SAP manages to solve the heaviness of its environment and the very high costs of its TCO before OpenERP reinforces its position by quickly meeting the needs for consolidation of its functionalities and by developing vertical solutions, then SAP will consolidate its leadership to the detriment of the open source world. In our opinion, this future should be settled within 5 years from now.

Part II

Project Approach

9. Introduction

A project approach is defined by the:

- Client scope;
- Solution to implement;
- Implementation methodology;
- Maturity of the client's organisation;
- Resources allocated by the client.

There is no "magic" approach but the consulting company can tailor a generic (template) approach in symbiosis with the client's project and culture. Whatever the solution, a generic approach should be followed.

The selected solution will impact the project implementation in many ways, by its approach, its constraints and its technical architecture.

The adage "Thinking Globally, Acting Locally" remains relevant to the present case.

This chapter will show you why and how the architecture will impact the implementation time.

10.Project approach for SAP: the Waterfall methodology

The centric and integrated architecture of SAP not only means "thinking globally – acting locally", it also means that it requires a detailed conceptual model of the "to be solution" between the thinking and the acting.

The approach usually used in that kind of project is often based on the Waterfall model.

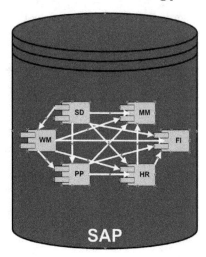

70. SAP's integrated architecture

The Waterfall model is a sequential design process in which progress is seen as flowing steadily downwards (like a waterfall) going through the phases of Conception, Initiation, Analysis, Design, Construction, Testing, Production/Implementation and Maintenance.

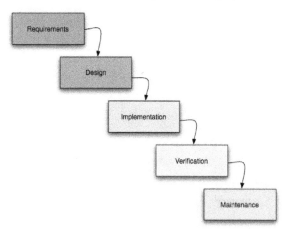

71. Waterfall Model

The idea is to implement an assembling of small units or cubes all fit into each other, like the cubic.

The Waterfall model is a static approach based on a static definition of the requirements. It works for static business or short time project. On a normal SAP implementation going from 9 months to … 3 years (without roll-out), it is difficult to freeze the client's business strategy. The main project risk of this methodology is that the delivered system fails to meet the client requirements due to the relatively large amount of time spent by teams between the Definition Study and the Implementation phases. This could greatly impact the management of the change requests. Even if a phasing approach can be proposed for large implementation taking more than 18 months before a go-life, the elapsed time of each phase will take at least 6 months.

However new costs arise when the project is split into phases. The first cost will be the overlap of project phases, the second one, the interface developed to support the transition phase with future modules and last but not least, the quality review of the data before the upload.

11.Project approach for OpenERP: the Spiral methodology

With new technologies such as web services, the applications design has completely changed. This transformation allows to have integrated processes going from a centralized and integrated architecture to a centralized and communicating architecture. This architecture is more agile by reusing objects for different concepts. This also means that the architecture can be supported by a less complex hardware.

The centric and communicating architecture of OpenERP also means "thinking globally – acting locally" but with more agility and flexibility. It enables an implementation with a reduced development cycle according to the Spiral methodology.

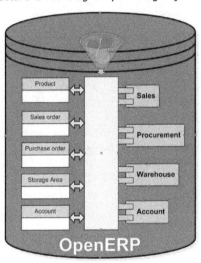

72. OpenERP: a centralised and communicating architecture

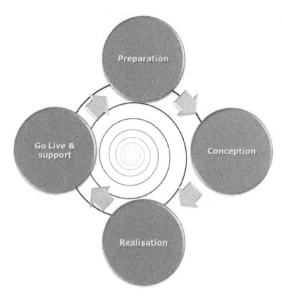

The Spiral model combines the idea of iterative projects (prototyping) with the systematic control aspects of the Waterfall model.

The Spiral model allows an incremental delivery of the solution through the spiral. The model includes risk management within the system customisation. Opposite to the Waterfall model, the documents are produced when they are needed, containing information required at that

73. The Spiral methodology

point in the process.

The goal of the model is to have a continuous stream of products available for users' review. It is a dynamic project approach necessary to maintain a momentum. It is like building a LEGO, a gradual construction starting on a solid foundation adding small blocs step by step, depending on the client's needs.

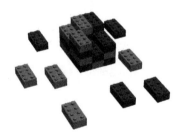

74. The Lego approach

OpenERP architecture and development in tree enable the LEGO approach

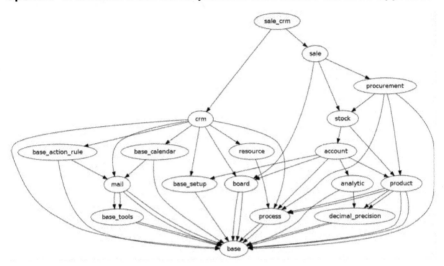

75. OpenERP architecture in tree

12.Conclusion

Both methodologies (Waterfall vs. Spiral) start with a global view of the client's needs, but OpenERP architecture and agility allow to give quicker tangible results to the client.

It makes it possible to easily evaluate the real progress of the project and to control its adequacy with the scope, deadlines and budget allocation, reducing the risk of implementing an unsuitable solution for the client.

Part III

The Open Eco-System

13. Business Model

The SAP Business model works like the other software vendors. Based on the official SAP figures[34] and information, we can put forward that SAP revenues is reducing in terms of services (9%) and increasing for its maintenance (4%) and license fees (5%). At the same time (between 2008 and 2010), the SAP global revenues have increased by 8%. On professional blogs, more and more clients criticize the maintenance costs strategy followed by SAP for a few years.

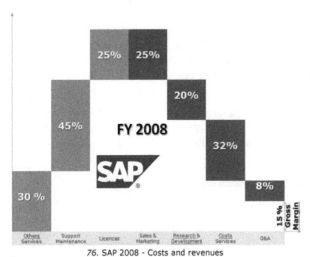

76. SAP 2008 - Costs and revenues

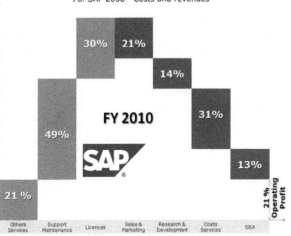

77. SAP 2010 - Costs and revenues

---

[34] http://www.sap.com/corporate-en/investors/reports/index.epx

If we look at the different open source software vendors, there are mainly two business models:

1. Releasing a light and open source version of the product and selling "non open source" modules with additional features, like SugarCRM, OpenBravo or Compiere, for instance;

2. Having 2 versions: an open source edition and a "non open" one that differ in some areas: Alfresco only releases bug fixes in the "non open" edition, MySQL has editions with different performances, and Magento has more features in the "non open" edition.

At OpenERP, they believe in open source and they have selected a third option: releasing everything for free. They have neither choosen the "Light Open Source Version" nor the "Non Open Edition" model. OpenERP publishes then the software for free (with no licenses cost) under the GNU Affero General Public License (GNU AGPL)[35].

Free as in freedom, not free as in free services.

OpenERP's sources of revenue necessary to finance the development and maintenance of its software are:

- **Online offer** (SaaS)[36]: to finance hosting, maintenance and OpenERP R&D;
- **OpenERP's Enterprise Contract**: to finance the maintenance and R&D. This contract can be considered as a warranty because the offered services cover not only the maintenance and the bug fixes (support level 2) but also the software upgrade with data conversion for the standard and certified modules. Concerning the bug fixes included in the OpenERP's Enterprise Contract, community members can report a bug on Launchpad[37] (the OpenERP community platform) and the development team will try to fix it. But if you need to interact directly with OpenERP or if you need a guarantee of response time, you will be charged for this extra service;
- **Partnership contract** (ready, silver or gold);
- **Services for partners or customers**: to finance the service team (trainers, partner managers, pre-sales support, etc.). OpenERP proposes training sessions on the functional and technical aspects of the solution. OpenERP can also provide developers to build new functionalities not covered by the community's modules.

---

[35] The **GNU Affero General Public License** is a free, copyleft license for software and other kinds of works, specifically designed to ensure cooperation with the community in the case of network server software. http://www.gnu.org/licenses/agpl-3.0.html
[36] http://www.openerp.com/online/
[37] https://launchpad.net/~openerp/+related-software

So, the OpenERP business model follows the SAP Business model except for the licences revenues.

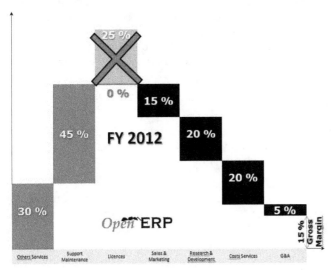

78. OpenERP Cost and Revenue Target model 2012

The OpenERP business model is supported by the organisation around the software vendor.

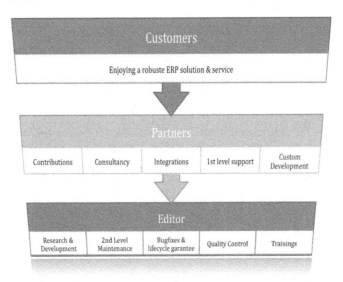

13.1.   The software vendor

The OpenERP team organises and structures the development/deployment of the new modules and releases of the solution. The OpenERP team is dedicated to verifying the quality of the development before integrating new functionalities into the OpenERP kernel. Today, there are around 1745 modules inside the community covering all the ERP's functionalities such as: Accounting, Stock Management, HR, CRM, Procurement, Sales, etc.

13.2.   The partners

The partners are also part of the OpenERP's marketing approach. Currently, OpenERP doesn't spend much money on marketing. The local marketing development is a partner's task.

The partners also contribute to the OpenERP solution development in the open source mode. They provide consultancy services (functional & technical), integration services in the client's IT environment, 1st level support and when necessary development of specific functionalities.

13.3.   The clients

The clients implementing OpenERP are advised to buy OpenERP's Enterprise contract, which is the software vendor's warranty. These clients can request consulting services from a partner

The OpenERP business model benefits a lot from its active community (marketing and sales) and their contributions (new features development). The community is great and OpenERP values its work. So, OpenERP also has to help members of the community to understand OpenERP's solution, how to contribute, etc. That is why OpenERP launched on Launchpad, the **Mementos**, a collaborative development platform where community managers work with community contributors, etc. Here is what you can find on the OpenERP.com website[38]. The same applies for migrations. Migrations in all ERP software are very complex. OpenERP wants to simplify this process while actively supporting the client. Even if upgrading remains a whole project, OpenERP has decided to include the migration service in its Enterprise Contract so that every client can easily upgrade and benefits from the new features. This is also a way to make sure that OpenERP's partners and clients will not face unexpected costs when a new version is released.

---

[38] More information about the open source model of OpenERP: http://bit.ly/openmodel

Part IV

Conclusion

This book shows the maturity of the OpenERP solution, the project approach used in order to configure the solution as well as the eco-system guaranteeing its viability compared to our reference point: SAP, leader on the ERP market.

The maturity acquired by OpenERP can be appreciated from two points of view: the maturity of the solution (the Product Life Cycle) and the maturity of the market (the profile of the client).

In the Product Life Cycle, OpenERP is in the growth phase. Indeed, the basic developments are done. The product was launched 8 years ago. Today, the product is stable and its quality is recognised. The new modules and the version updates bring new functionalities, improve the performance and reinforce the integration of existing functionalities. The software vendor plans to launch a long term service version (LTS) every 18 months, and a new version every 6 months. The staff and the number of OpenERP partners exponentially grow, with a turnover which doubles each year for two years now.

As far as the type of client who acquires OpenERP is concerned, we are in a transition phase. In the acquisition process of the product, every client is sensitive to its quality, its reliability, the viability of the software vendor, and to the guarantees provided in case of troubles as well. Most of the clients ("Early Majority Adopters" in the Rogers Innovation Curve) wait until an emerging product has been fully tried and tested by the innovative and visionary clients more willing to take some risks ("Early Adopters").

Beside the proprietary world, known and recognized for the guarantees it offers, the world of the open source is still little known by comparison with its use. Most of the IT departments (back office) of organisations use open source products on the majority of their servers: FTP server, DHCP, internet (APACHE), database (MySQL, PostgresQL), and for the virtualisation of their machines (Virtual Box) as well, etc. The open source remains a segment of products for "IT specialists". Even if several free office suite exist (Openoffice for example) offering functionalities convenient for most of the users (front office), they are not widely used. It is the same for the mailboxes (ZIMBRA, THUNDERBIRD, etc.). Only the open source web browsers are widely adopted for their user-friendliness (Google chrome, Firefox, Opera, etc.).

But the world changes. The recognition of the open source world is in full growth, going even to be imposed on organizations in their choice for a solution. For example, the European and the local public institutions are constrained by law to consider in their various projects the open source solutions before considering the proprietary ones. There is, for instance, a service within the European Parliament in charge of evaluating, selecting, adapting and supporting the open source solutions. The clients who plan to get all or part of the OpenERP solution have, today, the sufficient guarantees that the product and the software vendor are safe values. And it is only the beginning since the number and the size of the projects known in the pipe are in full growth.

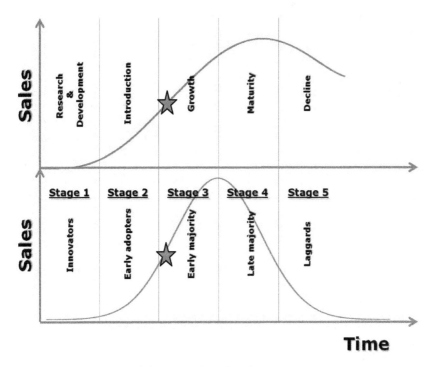

79. OpenERP Product Life Cycle & Adoption

OpenERP is facing new challenges within the "Early Majority" phase. These challenges concern various domains that have to be tackled by OpenERP in order to keep on progessing.

The commercial approach must be addressed to the Business by Business experts and no longer to the IT by IT experts.

The project approach must be re-orientated. Until now, the installation of OpenERP is usually regarded as being within the competence of the IT experts. It is a challenge for both the Business and the IT. The business expert must lead the client to adopt the most standard solution (best practices) in different dimensions while respecting the possible specificities of the client's core business; that is to say, processes, security, reporting, compliancy, governance, training, taxes, project management, etc. As for the IT expert, he will go together with the client in the installation, the integration of the solution in the IT landscape, the configuration of reports, the safety and the creation or the adaptation of functionalities specific to the client's business. Moreover, the dimension too often considered as optional, namely the "change management" yet represents a key success factor. The client must surround himself with business experts capable of going with the organizational changes, from the requirements definition to the final solution takeover. Sometimes, it happens that because the product is free, simple of use and the code open, people tend to believe that they can easily implement it by themselves without any specific expertise. When it turns out to be disappointing, it is in the human nature to question the product instead of the competences required to make the project a success.

From a functional point of view, OpenERP must extend its industry solution offer by integrating the specific requirements of some specific sectors. OpenERP must also keep on developing new functionalities expected by the clients (for instance: Advanced Treasury Management, Budgetary Management for Public Sector, etc.)

OpenERP must also remain watchful on the current or possible evolution of its competitors. Today, some proprietary programs extend their offers with open source programs such as for example Oracle with VirtualBox. What would happen if the proprietary programs rooted for a long time in their market decide to transform their licenses purchase offer into a single maintenance offer? How to approach the technological change that the proprietary platforms could anticipate so as to meet the future needs of the users?

Our vision

Today, it's the era of apps (Ipod, Iphone, Ipad ...) and networks (Facebook, Twitter ...) easily connecting more and more people. The new generation already apprehends in a totally different way the world of information, the tasks execution and the messaging. We already know that email usage will remain but decrease so as to be replaced by social networking for personal communication.

The world of tomorrow will be dematerialized. The personal computer (PC) will be used only by some specialists to maintain operational dematerialized environments and the ERP will no longer exist as a monolithic structure. The many support activities will be automatically initiated and controlled by neuronal systems learning from their mistakes and sharing their experiences with the other computers in a viral and community way. The activities with no added-value which consume time and money will disappear. Companies will then be able to concentrate on their main activities: production/service, sales and R&D. The future neuronal computers will have nothing to prove but rise, give and exchange together without emotion or conflict.

Are we still far from this new turning point, knowing that IBM has just released its first neuronal processor which includes an error learning process, like any human being?

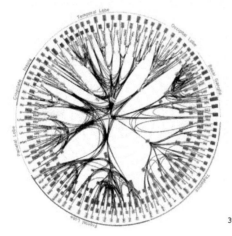

39

80. IBM produces first working chips modeled on the human brain

39 http://www.iheartchaos.com/post/9125189787/ibm-produces-first-working-chips-modeled-on-the-human

Illustrations Table

Annex

ERP[40] Definition

Enterprise resource planning (ERP) systems integrate internal and external management information across an entire organization, embracing finance/accounting, manufacturing, sales and service, client relationship management, etc. ERP systems automate this activity with an integrated software application. Its purpose is to facilitate the flow of information between all business functions inside the boundaries of the organization and manage the connections to outside stakeholders.

ERP systems can run on a variety of hardware and network configurations, typically employing a database as a repository for information.

ERP systems typically include the following characteristics:

•Integrated system that operates in real time (or next to real time), without relying on periodic updates;

•Common database, which supports all applications;

•Consistent look and feel throughout each module;

•Installation of the system without elaborate application/data integration by the Information Technology (IT) department.

---

40 http://en.wikipedia.org/wiki/Enterprise_resource_planning#Characteristics

Evaluation Table

Functional Domain: Business Functional domain

- DSP OE   OpenERP domain Weighted score
- DSP SAP   SAP domain Weighted score

Module: Major group of functionalities into the Business functional domain

- MSP OE   OpenERP module Weighted score
- MSP SAP   SAP module Weighted score
- MMS OE   OpenERP module score
- MMS SAP   SAP module score
- Pond.   Weight applied to the module score

Functionality: Functionality scored

- FSP OE   OpenERP functionality Weighted score
- FSP SAP   SAP functionality Weighted score
- Ponderation Weight applied to the functionality score
- OE Score   OpenERP Estimated score related to client's expectation
- SAP Score   SAP Estimated score related to client's expectation

Accounting & Financial Management   DSP OE: 79% DSP SAP: 98

agement   MSP OE: 75% MSP SAP: 100% Pond.:   100% MMS OE: 75% MMS SAP:

Functionality	FSP OE	FSP SAP	Ponderation	OE Score	SAP Score
Accept for multiple invoices for the same asset	100%	100%	100%	100%	100%
Possibility to amortize the same asset in different ways	100%	100%	100%	100%	100%
Insurance facility on Assets	0%	100%	100%	0%	100%
IFRS compliant assets	0%	100%	100%	0%	100%
Availability of inventories of different assets	100%	100%	100%	100%	100%
Availability of calculating Depreciation	100%	100%	100%	100%	100%
Automatic generation of accounting entries based on assets	100%	100%	100%	100%	100%
Availability of an asset management system	100%	100%	110%	100%	100%

nents   MSP OE: 105% MSP SAP: 105% Pond.:   100% MMS OE: 105% MMS SAP:

Functionality	FSP OE	FSP SAP	Ponderation	OE Score	SAP Score
Support for write-off in payments	100%	100%	100%	100%	100%
Import entries in bank statements from invoices	100%	100%	90%	100%	100%
Encode entries in statement or load existing entries in	100%	100%	90%	100%	100%
Availability of a bank statement view	100%	100%	100%	100%	100%

MSP OE: 75% MSP SAP: 100% Pond.:   100% MMS OE: 75% MMS SAP:

Functionality	FSP OE	FSP SAP	Ponderation	OE Score	SAP Score
Integration to analytic accounting	75%	100%	100%	75%	100%
Consolidations and views by departments, project or budget	75%	100%	100%	75%	100%

iscal years   MSP OE: 105% MSP SAP: 105% Pond.:   100% MMS OE: 105% MMS SAP:

Functionality	FSP OE	FSP SAP	Ponderation	OE Score	SAP Score
Automatic generation of entries when closing a fiscal year	100%	100%	100%	100%	100%
ility to generate closing entries without closing a fiscal year	100%	100%	90%	100%	100%
Ability to cancel closing entries without closing a fiscal year	100%	100%	90%	100%	100%
Manages reconciliation of invoices on closed fiscal years	100%	100%	100%	100%	100%

tomers Follow-Up   MSP OE: 107%   MSP SAP: 120%   Pond.:   120%   MMS OE: 89%   MM

Functionality	FSP OE	FSP SAP	Ponderation	OE Score	SAP
Automatic emails sent based on follow-ups	75%	100%	100%	75%	10
Support for multiple payment terms	60%	100%	100%	60%	10
Automatic follow-ups with unlimited levels	100%	100%	100%	100%	10
Ability to define default payment terms on suppliers	100%	100%	100%	100%	10
Ability to define default payment terms on customers	100%	100%	100%	100%	10
Generations of letters for the customer according to the level	100%	100%	100%	100%	10

t encoding of entries MSP OE: 89%   MSP SAP: 89%   Pond.:   100%   MMS OE: 89%   MM

Functionality	FSP OE	FSP SAP	Ponderation	OE Score	SAP
Number of keys to encode an invoice entry <10	100%	100%	100%	100%	10
Full keyboard support	100%	100%	160%	100%	10
Encoding by entries and entries lines	100%	100%	100%	100%	10
Bank statement encoding facilities	100%	100%	100%	100%	10
Automatic computation of taxes and analytic entries	100%	100%	100%	100%	10

cibility   MSP OE: 100%   MSP SAP: 100%   Pond.:   100%   MMS OE: 100%   MM

Functionality	FSP OE	FSP SAP	Ponderation	OE Score	SAP
Ability to define constraints on accounts to use depending on	100%	100%	100%	100%	10
Ability to close a journal	100%	100%	100%	100%	10
Ability to close a period (not a complete fiscal year)	100%	100%	100%	100%	10
Ability to configure accounts and taxes on products	100%	100%	100%	100%	10
Ability to define accounting rules depending on partners and	100%	100%	100%	100%	10
Ability to change all operations: product's quantities,	100%	100%	100%	100%	10
Ability to define customized views for entries per journal	100%	100%	100%	100%	10
Unlimitted size for account numbers	100%	100%	100%	100%	10
Reorganisation of proposed manufacturing orders and work	100%	100%	100%	100%	10
If an entry is confirmed, you can change non legal values	100%	100%	100%	100%	10
Access rights with different posting groups per journal	100%	100%	100%	100%	10

Accounting & Financial Management   DSP OE: 79% DSP SAP: 9

	MSP OE:	100%	MSP SAP:	100%	Pond.:	100%	MMS OE:	100%	MMS SAP:
Functionality		FSP OE	FSP SAP		Ponderation		OE Score		SAP Score
Ability to easily cancel any scheduled operation		100%	100%		100%		100%		100%
Ability to browse the chart of account as a hiearchy (tree		100%	100%		100%		100%		100%
ility to confirm draft entries so that you can not change them		100%	100%		100%		100%		100%

ntries   MSP OE: 66% MSP SAP: 105% Pond.:   100% MMS OE: 66% MMS SAP:

Functionality	FSP OE	FSP SAP	Ponderation	OE Score	SAP Score
Possibility to define recurring operations for automatic	75%	100%	90%	75%	100%
Ability to call a model when encoding entries	100%	100%	90%	100%	100%
Ability to put computation formulae in model of entries	0%	100%	110%	0%	100%
Availability to define model of entries for recurring operations	75%	100%	90%	75%	100%

pany Support MSP OE: 75% MSP SAP: 100% Pond.:   100% MMS OE: 75% MMS SAP:

Functionality	FSP OE	FSP SAP	Ponderation	OE Score	SAP Score
Support for multiple chart of accounts for multiple companies	60%	100%	100%	60%	100%
Accept all reports on consolidated chart of accounts	100%	100%	100%	100%	100%
Account sharing between companies	60%	100%	100%	60%	100%
Client sharing between companies	60%	100%	100%	60%	100%
Support for consolidation of multiple chart of accounts in real	100%	100%	100%	100%	100%
Support for different fiscal years for each company	75%	100%	100%	75%	100%

ency Support MSP OE: 74% MSP SAP: 100% Pond.:   100% MMS OE: 74% MMS SAP:

Functionality	FSP OE	FSP SAP	Ponderation	OE Score	SAP Score
Possibility to automatically update daily currencies rate	50%	100%	100%	50%	100%
Support for average rate when crediting bank accounts	100%	100%	100%	100%	100%
Support for current rate when crediting bank accounts	100%	100%	100%	100%	100%
Automatic proposition of currencies amount based on account	60%	100%	100%	60%	100%
Support for multiple-currencies in reconciliation process	60%	100%	100%	60%	100%
Support for multiple currencies	75%	100%	100%	75%	100%

Management   MSP OE: 82% MSP SAP: 100% Pond.:   100% MMS OE: 82% MMS SAP:

Functionality	FSP OE	FSP SAP	Ponderation	OE Score	SAP Score

ient Management MSP OE: 82% MSP SAP: 100% Pond.: 100% MMS OE: 82% MMS

Functionality	FSP OE	FSP SAP	Ponderation	OE Score	SAP S
Support for the new european standard SEPA for electronic	100%	100%	100%	100%	100%
Generate eletronic files for bank payments	100%	100%	100%	100%	100%
Different users for preparation and execution of payments	100%	100%	100%	100%	100%
Availability of a system to prepare payments based on	100%	100%	100%	100%	100%
Support for partial payments	100%	100%	100%	100%	100%
Print checks based on payment preparations	0%	100%	100%	0%	100%
Ability to automatically import payments into bank	75%	100%	100%	75%	100%

nciliation process MSP OE: 99% MSP SAP: 103% Pond.: 100% MMS OE: 99% MMS

Functionality	FSP OE	FSP SAP	Ponderation	OE Score	SAP S
Availability of a tool to automatically detect reconciliations	75%	100%	100%	75%	100%
Automatic reconciliation when several partial closes the	100%	100%	100%	100%	100%
Support for partial reconciliation	100%	100%	90%	100%	100%
Ability to unreconcile entries for some users	100%	100%	90%	100%	100%
Ability to reconcile from accounting entries	100%	100%	100%	100%	100%
Ability to reconcile from statements	100%	100%	100%	100%	100%
Ability to reconcile from invoice payments	100%	100%	100%	100%	100%

sury Management MSP OE: 0% MSP SAP: 90% Pond.: 120% MMS OE: 0% MMS

Functionality	FSP OE	FSP SAP	Ponderation	OE Score	SAP S
Availability of a treasury forecast report	0%	100%	100%	0%	100%
Treasury forecasts based on sales, purchases and invoices	0%	100%	100%	0%	100%
Treasury forecasts based on CRM opportunities	0%	0%	100%	0%	0%
Dynamic and graphical forecasts	0%	100%	100%	0%	100%

ns Management MSP OE: 92% MSP SAP: 110% Pond.: 110% MMS OE: 83% MMS

Functionality	FSP OE	FSP SAP	Ponderation	OE Score	SAP S
Support for attached documents describing the problem	100%	100%	100%	100%	100%

After-Sales Services DSP OE: 96% DSP SAP: 10(

nagement	MSP OE:	92%	MSP SAP:	110%	Pond.:	110%	MMS OE:	83%	MMS SAP:

Functionality	FSP OE	FSP SAP	Ponderation	OE Score	SAP Score
Support for corrective and preventive actions in claims	100%	100%	100%	100%	100%
Integrates suppliers claims management	0%	100%	100%	0%	100%
Integrates customers claims management	100%	100%	100%	100%	100%
Attach claims to lots, products and partners	100%	100%	100%	100%	100%
Traceability of the discussion and actions on the claim	100%	100%	100%	100%	100%

nagement	MSP OE:	110%	MSP SAP:	110%	Pond.:	110%	MMS OE:	100%	MMS SAP:

Functionality	FSP OE	FSP SAP	Ponderation	OE Score	SAP Score
Integration of the quality manual	100%	100%	100%	100%	100%
Support for alerts and warnings based on customizable	100%	100%	100%	100%	100%
Support for corrective and preventive actions In quality	100%	100%	100%	100%	100%
Visual integration of company processes as graphs	100%	100%	100%	100%	100%

anagement	MSP OE:	110%	MSP SAP:	110%	Pond.:	110%	MMS OE:	100%	MMS SAP:

Functionality	FSP OE	FSP SAP	Ponderation	OE Score	SAP Score
Manages repairs at customer location	100%	100%	100%	100%	100%
Manages reparation in the warehouse	100%	100%	100%	100%	100%
Traceability of all operations on the lot	100%	100%	100%	100%	100%
Automatic invoicing of raw materials and products	100%	100%	100%	100%	100%
Automatic invoicing of services or hours spent on repairs	100%	100%	100%	100%	100%
Manages reception of defect products and deliveries	100%	100%	100%	100%	100%

Management	MSP OE:	100%	MSP SAP:	100%	Pond.:	100%	MMS OE:	100%	MMS SAP:

Functionality	FSP OE	FSP SAP	Ponderation	OE Score	SAP Score
Automatic re-invoicing of products/services based on	100%	100%	100%	100%	100%
Waranties limit computation based on lots	100%	100%	100%	100%	100%

Analytic accounting DSP OE: 85% DSP SAP: 10

tructure	MSP OE:	88%	MSP SAP:	100%	Pond.:	100%	MMS OE:	88%	MMS SAP:

Functionality	FSP OE	FSP SAP	Ponderation	OE Score	SAP Score

Analytic accounting

DSP OE: 85% DSP SAP:

ytic Structure   MSP OE: 88% MSP SAP: 100% Pond.: 100% MMS OE: 88% MMS

Functionality	FSP OE	FSP SAP	Ponderation	OE Score	SAP S
Each analytic account can work with multiple currencies	50%	100%	100%	50%	100
Each analytic plan can be hierarchised (tree structure)	100%	100%	100%	100%	100
Support for multiple analytic plans	100%	100%	100%	100%	100
Support for an unlimited number of plans and hierarchy	100%	100%	100%	100%	100

matic integration   MSP OE: 86% MSP SAP: 94% Pond.: 90% MMS OE: 96% MMS

others components

Functionality	FSP OE	FSP SAP	Ponderation	OE Score	SAP S
Manufacturing orders can create analytic entries costs	100%	100%	90%	100%	100
Supplier and customer invoices generates analytic entries	100%	100%	100%	100%	100
Employees leaves/hollidays can generate analytic costs	100%	100%	100%	100%	100
Assets are integrated with analytic accounting	60%	100%	90%	60%	100
Time spent on a task can generate analytic entries	100%	100%	100%	100%	100

ies encoding   MSP OE: 80% MSP SAP: 103% Pond.: 100% MMS OE: 80% MMS

Functionality	FSP OE	FSP SAP	Ponderation	OE Score	SAP S
Support for end-of-campaign discounts	50%	100%	100%	50%	100
Support for end-of-year discounts	50%	100%	100%	50%	100
Support for manually encoding of analytic entries	100%	100%	100%	100%	100
Support for model of analytic distributions	75%	100%	90%	75%	100
Support for promotions pricelists	100%	100%	100%	100%	100
One financial entry can be splitted in several analytic lines	100%	100%	100%	100%	100
Ability to set a discount per sale/Purchase order line	50%	100%	100%	50%	100
Support for analytic entries without financial entries counter-	100%	100%	90%	100%	100

ures   MSP OE: 80% MSP SAP: 120% Pond.: 120% MMS OE: 67% MMS

Functionality	FSP OE	FSP SAP	Ponderation	OE Score	SAP S
Integrated with project management (planning, costs of	100%	100%	100%	100%	100
Ability to consolidates accounts from multiple companies	50%	100%	100%	50%	100
Automatically propose the account based on user, product,	50%	100%	100%	50%	100

Analytic accounting

DSP OE: 85% DSP SAP: 103

MSP OE: 80% MSP SAP: 120% Pond.: 120% MMS OE: 67% MMS SAP:

Functionality	FSP OE	FSP SAP	Ponderation	OE Score	SAP Score
Ability to automatically reinvoice costs	100%	100%	100%	100%	100%
Support for multi-company environment	50%	100%	100%	50%	100%
Ability to link users to different products based on	50%	100%	100%	50%	100%

MSP OE: 98% MSP SAP: 107% Pond.: 100% MMS OE: 98% MMS SAP:

Functionality	FSP OE	FSP SAP	Ponderation	OE Score	SAP Score
Ability to compute the theorical revenue based on costs and	75%	100%	100%	75%	100%
Availability of graphical dashboards and indicators	100%	100%	90%	100%	100%
Support for cross-reports between several analytic plans	100%	100%	90%	100%	100%

CRM & SRM

DSP OE: 82% DSP SAP: 91

...anagement MSP OE: 85% MSP SAP: 100% Pond.: 100% MMS OE: 85% MMS SAP:

/partners)

Functionality	FSP OE	FSP SAP	Ponderation	OE Score	SAP Score
Prospects management and conversion to customers	100%	100%	100%	100%	100%
Multiple relations between enterprises (accounts) and	100%	100%	100%	100%	100%
Integration with phone central (VOIP)	60%	100%	100%	60%	100%
Automatic segmentations of accounts	80%	100%	100%	80%	100%

...ration MSP OE: 50% MSP SAP: 75% Pond.: 100% MMS OE: 50% MMS SAP:

Functionality	FSP OE	FSP SAP	Ponderation	OE Score	SAP Score
Evolution plugin to push important emails in the software	0%	100%	100%	0%	100%
...hunderbird plugin to push important emails in the software	100%	0%	100%	100%	0%
Synchronisation of contacts with Outlook	50%	100%	100%	50%	100%
Outlook plugin to push important emails in the software	50%	100%	100%	50%	100%

MSP OE: 94% MSP SAP: 100% Pond.: 100% MMS OE: 94% MMS SAP:

Functionality	FSP OE	FSP SAP	Ponderation	OE Score	SAP Score
Calendar per day,week,month,year	75%	100%	100%	75%	100%
Drag & Drop in the calendar of events	100%	100%	100%	100%	100%
Drag and drop between opportunities for prioritization	100%	100%	100%	100%	100%

Domain:	**CRM & SRM**			DSP OE:	82% DSP SAP:	
onomy	MSP OE: 94% MSP SAP:	100% Pond.:		100% MMS OE:	94% MM	

	Functionality	FSP OE	FSP SAP	Ponderation	OE Score	SAP
	Accessibility of all information in forms	100%	100%	100%	100%	10
egrated Webmail	MSP OE: 100% MSP SAP: 100% Pond.:			90% MMS OE:	111% MM	
	Functionality	FSP OE	FSP SAP	Ponderation	OE Score	SAP
	Support for IMAP	100%	100%	90%	100%	10
	Customizable screens for business logic	100%	100%	90%	100%	10
	Ergonomy: drag&drop, ajax enabled	100%	100%	90%	100%	10
	Support for POP	100%	100%	90%	100%	10
	Search, rules, hyerarchical folders	100%	100%	90%	100%	10
egrations	MSP OE: 67% MSP SAP: 67% Pond.:			100% MMS OE:	67% MM	
	Functionality	FSP OE	FSP SAP	Ponderation	OE Score	SAP
	Integration with Outlook for mails and contacts	50%	100%	100%	50%	10
	Web portal	50%	100%	100%	50%	10
	Integration with Thunderbird for mails and contacts	100%	0%	100%	100%	0
ds management	MSP OE: 83% MSP SAP: 111% Pond.:			100% MMS OE:	83% MM	
	Functionality	FSP OE	FSP SAP	Ponderation	OE Score	SAP
	Wizard to simplify mass importation of prospects	75%	100%	90%	75%	10
	Creation of accounts and opportunities based on leads	75%	100%	90%	75%	10
	Automatic creation of leads based on incoming email	100%	100%	90%	100%	10
	Automatic creation of leads based on a website form	50%	100%	90%	50%	10
keting Campaigns	MSP OE: 68% MSP SAP: 60% Pond.:			90% MMS OE:	75% MM	
agement	Functionality	FSP OE	FSP SAP	Ponderation	OE Score	SAP
	Integration with Ms. Word for mass mailing preparation	50%	100%	100%	50%	10
	Integration with OpenOffice for mass mailing preparation	100%	0%	100%	100%	0
	Segmentation tools for accounts	75%	100%	100%	75%	10
ortunities	MSP OE: 92% MSP SAP: 100% Pond.:			100% MMS OE:	92% MM	
agement	Functionality	FSP OE	FSP SAP	Ponderation	OE Score	SAP
	Create quotations or sales based on opportunities	100%	100%	100%	100%	10

n:	**CRM & SRM**			DSP OE:	82% DSP SAP: ![]9
ities	MSP OE: 92% MSP SAP:	100% Pond.:	100% MMS OE:	92% MMS SAP:	

Functionality	FSP OE	FSP SAP	Ponderation	OE Score	SAP Score
Ability to mass import phone calls	100%	100%	100%	100%	100%
Ability to make phone calls	100%	100%	100%	100%	100%
Ability to integrate opportunities and actions on the calendar	100%	100%	100%	100%	100%
Ability to define rules to route phone calls management	50%	100%	100%	50%	100%
Ability to customize screens according to the business	100%	100%	100%	100%	100%

n:	**Customer & Supplier Portal**			DSP OE:	82% DSP SAP: ![]5
Portal	MSP OE: 73% MSP SAP:	48% Pond.:	90% MMS OE:	82% MMS SAP:	

Functionality	FSP OE	FSP SAP	Ponderation	OE Score	SAP Score
Customers can access his own sales orders and quotations	75%	50%	90%	75%	50%
Different access rights possible per customer	100%	100%	90%	100%	100%
Customers can work on their own projects and tasks	75%	50%	90%	75%	50%
Customers can access using a web interface	100%	75%	100%	100%	75%
Customers can access using an application to install	100%	0%	100%	100%	0%
Support for unlimited number of portals (resellers,	75%	25%	90%	75%	25%
ustomers can access their own documents using web-services	75%	50%	100%	75%	50%
Customers can access documents using a WebDav access	0%	0%	110%	0%	0%
Customers can access documents using a FTP access	100%	50%	100%	100%	50%
Customers can access and reprint his own invoices	100%	100%	90%	100%	100%
Ability to reorganise menus of the portal	75%	25%	90%	75%	25%
Ability to export any kind of document in the portal	75%	75%	90%	75%	75%
Ability to create and send new users based on a selection of	50%	25%	90%	50%	25%
Customers can have a restricted visibility on stock	75%	75%	90%	75%	75%
Customers can access his after-sales services and support	75%	50%	90%	75%	50%

Portal	MSP OE: 75% MSP SAP:	44% Pond.:	90% MMS OE:	83% MMS SAP:	

Functionality	FSP OE	FSP SAP	Ponderation	OE Score	SAP Score
Suppliers can access documents using a FTP access	100%	50%	90%	100%	50%

Domain: **Customer & Supplier Portal** DSP OE: 82% DSP SAP:

ier Portal MSP OE: 75% MSP SAP: 44% Pond.: 90% MMS OE: 83% MMS

Functionality	FSP OE	FSP SAP	Ponderation	OE Score	SAP Sc
Suppliers can have a restricted visibility on stock availabilities	75%	75%	90%	75%	75%
Suppliers can access using an application to install	100%	0%	90%	100%	0%
Suppliers can access using a web interface	100%	75%	90%	100%	75%
Suppliers can access documents using a WebDav access	0%	0%	90%	0%	0%
Suppliers can work on their own projects and tasks	75%	50%	90%	75%	50%
Suppliers can access and complete requests for quotations	75%	50%	90%	75%	50%
Suppliers can access their own documents using web-services	75%	50%	90%	75%	50%

Domain: **Direct Marketing** DSP OE: 72% DSP SAP:

paign management MSP OE: 80% MSP SAP: 85% Pond.: 90% MMS OE: 89% MMS

Functionality	FSP OE	FSP SAP	Ponderation	OE Score	SAP Sc
Tools to search and avoid deduplications of prospects	75%	75%	90%	75%	75%
Tools to manage mass importation of prospects	100%	100%	90%	100%	100%
Manage a complete workflow of events for a campaign	100%	100%	90%	100%	100%
Ability to track segments of cutomers through the campaign	75%	75%	90%	75%	75%
Ability to manage the retro-planning on an campaign	50%	75%	90%	50%	75%

based campaigns MSP OE: 0% MSP SAP: 0% Pond.: 75% MMS OE: 0% MMS

Functionality	FSP OE	FSP SAP	Ponderation	OE Score	SAP Sc
Email composition using HTML	0%	0%	100%	0%	0%
Ability to add trackers in emails for reporting	0%	0%	100%	0%	0%
Ability to add trackers on links provided in the email	0%	0%	100%	0%	0%

s management MSP OE: 85% MSP SAP: 95% Pond.: 100% MMS OE: 85% MMS

Functionality	FSP OE	FSP SAP	Ponderation	OE Score	SAP Sc
Ability to define a complete workflow of steps in an offer	100%	75%	100%	100%	75%
Ability to define products and marketing documents at each	75%	100%	100%	75%	100%
Ability to define re-useable campaigns	100%	100%	100%	100%	100%
Ability to manage multi-media campaigns (email, sms, paper)	100%	100%	100%	100%	100%

Direct Marketing DSP OE: 72% DSP SAP: 7

hagement MSP OE: 85% MSP SAP: 95% Pond.: 100% MMS OE: 85% MMS SAP:

Functionality	FSP OE	FSP SAP	Ponderation	OE Score	SAP Score
Ability to manage the retro-planning on an offer	50%	100%	100%	50%	100%

ed campaigns MSP OE: 94% MSP SAP: 69% Pond.: 100% MMS OE: 94% MMS SAP:

Functionality	FSP OE	FSP SAP	Ponderation	OE Score	SAP Score
Mass mailing merging and routing	100%	100%	100%	100%	100%
Barcode support for fast encoding of orders	75%	100%	100%	75%	100%
Complex layouts of mailings designed using Ms. or	100%	0%	100%	100%	0%
PDF generation of the mailings	100%	75%	100%	100%	75%

tions MSP OE: 50% MSP SAP: 100% Pond.: 100% MMS OE: 50% MMS SAP:

Functionality	FSP OE	FSP SAP	Ponderation	OE Score	SAP Score
Tools for automatic segmentations of customers or prospects	50%	100%	100%	50%	100%
Statistics reports on return answers per segments	50%	100%	100%	50%	100%

d campaigns MSP OE: 90% MSP SAP: 90% Pond.: 90% MMS OE: 100% MMS SAP:

Functionality	FSP OE	FSP SAP	Ponderation	OE Score	SAP Score
Connection available to an SMS gateway	100%	100%	100%	100%	100%

Document Management System DSP OE: 81% DSP SAP: 8

ity of MSP OE: 69% MSP SAP: 81% Pond.: 100% MMS OE: 69% MMS SAP:

s

Functionality	FSP OE	FSP SAP	Ponderation	OE Score	SAP Score
FTP access	100%	75%	90%	100%	75%
Web interface to browse documents	75%	75%	100%	75%	75%
Webdav access	0%	75%	110%	0%	75%
Email integration for incoming documents	100%	100%	100%	100%	100%

ices MSP OE: 92% MSP SAP: 83% Pond.: 100% MMS OE: 92% MMS SAP:

Functionality	FSP OE	FSP SAP	Ponderation	OE Score	SAP Score
Version control system	100%	100%	100%	100%	100%
Configurable rules to automatically process documents	75%	50%	100%	75%	50%
History of modifications	100%	100%	100%	100%	100%

Document Management System

sification of   MSP OE: 89% MSP SAP: 83% Pond.: 110% MMS OE: 81% MMS

ments

Functionality	FSP OE	FSP SAP	Ponderation	OE Score	SAP S
Automatic attachment of printed reports	75%	50%	100%	75%	50%
Classification of attached documents into folders	100%	100%	100%	100%	100
Automatic classification according to templates	50%	50%	100%	50%	50%
Ability to attach documents on any resource	100%	100%	100%	100%	100

gration   MSP OE: 63% MSP SAP: 88% Pond.: 100% MMS OE: 63% MMS

Functionality	FSP OE	FSP SAP	Ponderation	OE Score	SAP S
Single point of security management for DMS and ERP	100%	100%	100%	100%	100
Outlook integration to quickly add or get documents from	25%	75%	100%	25%	75%

rting   MSP OE: 83% MSP SAP: 83% Pond.: 100% MMS OE: 83% MMS

Functionality	FSP OE	FSP SAP	Ponderation	OE Score	SAP S
Statistics on Document Management System usage	100%	100%	90%	100%	100
Statistics on user's aceptability of the DMS	50%	50%	90%	50%	50%

ch of documents   MSP OE: 97% MSP SAP: 68% Pond.: 100% MMS OE: 97% MMS

Functionality	FSP OE	FSP SAP	Ponderation	OE Score	SAP S
Automatic indexation of images content (OCR)	75%	50%	100%	75%	50%
Search on content, metadata	100%	100%	100%	100%	100
Meta data support: project, account, user, status, version, ...	100%	100%	100%	100%	100
Automatic indexation of PDF's files contents	100%	75%	100%	100%	75%
Automatic indexation of Microsoft Office files contents	100%	75%	100%	100%	75%
Automatic indexation of OpenOffice files contents	100%	0%	90%	100%	0%

Human Ressources

ndances   MSP OE: 88% MSP SAP: 88% Pond.: 100% MMS OE: 88% MMS

Functionality	FSP OE	FSP SAP	Ponderation	OE Score	SAP S
Availability of interfaces with hardware material for	75%	75%	100%	75%	75%
Availability of an attendance management system	100%	100%	100%	100%	100

nses Tracking   MSP OE: 97% MSP SAP: 102% Pond.: 100% MMS OE: 97% MMS

Functionality	FSP OE	FSP SAP	Ponderation	OE Score	SAP S

Human Ressources

DSP OE: 78% **DSP SAP:** 99

racking MSP OE: 97% MSP SAP: 102% Pond.: 100% MMS OE: 97% MMS SAP:

Functionality	FSP OE	FSP SAP	Ponderation	OE Score	SAP Score
Ability to manage expense notes	100%	100%	100%	100%	100%
Allows employee without accounting knowledge to encode	100%	100%	90%	100%	100%
Automatic generation of expenses accounting entries	100%	100%	100%	100%	100%
Support for multi-currencies expenses	75%	100%	100%	75%	100%
Workflow: Draft -> Confirmed -> Approved Manager ->	100%	100%	100%	100%	100%
Ability to manage employee reimbursement	100%	100%	100%	100%	100%

Leaves MSP OE: 79% MSP SAP: 90% Pond.: 90% MMS OE: 88% MMS SAP:

Functionality	FSP OE	FSP SAP	Ponderation	OE Score	SAP Score
Integrated with analytic accounting for costs of leaves	100%	100%	100%	100%	100%
Integrated with enterprise calendar and planning	50%	100%	100%	50%	100%
Availability of a employee leave management system	100%	100%	100%	100%	100%
Workflow management: request holiday -> accepted by	100%	100%	100%	100%	100%

agement MSP OE: 50% MSP SAP: 150% Pond.: 160% MMS OE: 31% MMS SAP:

Functionality	FSP OE	FSP SAP	Ponderation	OE Score	SAP Score
Integration of payroll with employee's attendances	25%	100%	110%	25%	100%
Availability of a payroll system	25%	100%	100%	25%	100%
Automatic generation of Payroll accounting entries	50%	100%	110%	50%	100%

gement MSP OE: 83% MSP SAP: 100% Pond.: 90% MMS OE: 93% MMS SAP:

Functionality	FSP OE	FSP SAP	Ponderation	OE Score	SAP Score
Availability of skills management features on employees	75%	100%	90%	75%	100%
Employees periodical evaluation forms	100%	100%	90%	100%	100%
Reports on enterprise consolidated skills	75%	100%	90%	75%	100%

MSP OE: 101% MSP SAP: 101% Pond.: 100% MMS OE: 101% MMS SAP:

Functionality	FSP OE	FSP SAP	Ponderation	OE Score	SAP Score
Ability to encode timesheets by hours	100%	100%	100%	100%	100%
Validation workflow on timesheets by periods	100%	100%	100%	100%	100%
Integration of timesheets with tasks	100%	100%	100%	100%	100%

Domain: **Human Ressources** DSP OE: 78% DSP SAP:

esheets MSP OE: 101% MSP SAP: 101% Pond.: 100% MMS OE: 101% MM

Functionality	FSP OE	FSP SAP	Ponderation	OE Score	SAP
Integration of timesheets with planning	100%	100%	100%	100%	10
Integration of timesheets with analytic or cost accounting	100%	100%	100%	100%	10
Ability to encode timesheets by days	100%	100%	100%	100%	10
Integration of timesheets with attendances for comparisons	100%	100%	90%	100%	10

Domain: **Manufacturing Management** DSP OE: 62% DSP SAP:

ch Process MSP OE: 40% MSP SAP: 85% Pond.: 100% MMS OE: 40% MM

Functionality	FSP OE	FSP SAP	Ponderation	OE Score	SAP
Ability to define down anticipated life	0%	100%	100%	0%	10
Define substitutes for parts of process	100%	100%	100%	100%	10
Batch sizes and underlying ingredients can be adjusted	100%	100%	100%	100%	10
Batch analysis for economical production	0%	75%	100%	0%	7
Adjustment of batches by region and/or country	0%	50%	100%	0%	5

t-Practices MSP OE: 78% MSP SAP: 91% Pond.: 100% MMS OE: 78% MM

Functionality	FSP OE	FSP SAP	Ponderation	OE Score	SAP
Kanban support with stock level computation per location	75%	75%	100%	75%	7
Bar code support on products and lots	75%	75%	100%	75%	7
Central point of management for all exceptions	100%	100%	100%	100%	10
Just-in-Time Support in Manufacturing	75%	100%	100%	75%	10
Management of assembly lines per location	100%	100%	100%	100%	10
Multiple plants management	100%	100%	100%	100%	10
Real time detection of bottle necks	25%	100%	100%	25%	10
Bar code support for operations	75%	75%	100%	75%	7

onomy and ease of MSP OE: 75% MSP SAP: 75% Pond.: 100% MMS OE: 75% MM

Functionality	FSP OE	FSP SAP	Ponderation	OE Score	SAP
Gantt manipulation of manufacturing orders	75%	75%	100%	75%	7
Gantt manipulation of work orders	75%	75%	100%	75%	7

and ease of   MSP OE: 75% MSP SAP: 75% Pond.:   100% MMS OE: 75% MMS SAP:

Functionality	FSP OE	FSP SAP	Ponderation	OE Score	SAP Score
Support for Drag&Drop for priorities and routings	75%	75%	100%	75%	75%

n   MSP OE: 88% MSP SAP: 81% Pond.:   100% MMS OE: 88% MMS SAP:

Functionality	FSP OE	FSP SAP	Ponderation	OE Score	SAP Score
Alerts on stock levels by email	100%	50%	100%	100%	50%
Sub-contracting of work orders management	100%	100%	100%	100%	100%
Manufacuring simulations in quotations or sales orders	50%	75%	100%	50%	75%
Integration of services in manufacturing orders	100%	100%	100%	100%	100%

agement   MSP OE: 94% MSP SAP: 94% Pond.:   100% MMS OE: 94% MMS SAP:

Functionality	FSP OE	FSP SAP	Ponderation	OE Score	SAP Score
Alerts and visibility on lots availability	100%	100%	100%	100%	100%
Bar code support for lots	75%	75%	100%	75%	75%
Lots on palets/boxes	100%	100%	100%	100%	100%
Lots number on manufactured products or raw materials	100%	100%	100%	100%	100%

tures   MSP OE: 75% MSP SAP: 96% Pond.:   100% MMS OE: 75% MMS SAP:

Functionality	FSP OE	FSP SAP	Ponderation	OE Score	SAP Score
Stock forecasts	25%	100%	100%	25%	100%
Support for products of substitution	75%	100%	100%	75%	100%
Support for sales packs	100%	100%	100%	100%	100%
Support of substition of bill of materials	50%	75%	100%	50%	75%
Multi-Level Bill of Materials support	100%	100%	100%	100%	100%
Make-to-Stock / Make-to-Order support	100%	100%	100%	100%	100%

atures   MSP OE: 0% MSP SAP: 75% Pond.:   120% MMS OE: 0% MMS SAP:

Functionality	FSP OE	FSP SAP	Ponderation	OE Score	SAP Score
Support for simulations of procurements	0%	50%	100%	0%	50%
Master Production Schedule	0%	75%	100%	0%	75%

ntenance   MSP OE: 50% MSP SAP: 100% Pond.:   100% MMS OE: 50% MMS SAP:

Functionality	FSP OE	FSP SAP	Ponderation	OE Score	SAP Score

omain: **Manufacturing Management** DSP OE: 62% DSP SAP:

Maintenance MSP OE: 50% MSP SAP: 100% Pond.: 100% MMS OE: 50% MMS

Functionality	FSP OE	FSP SAP	Ponderation	OE Score	SAP S
Preventive and breakdown maintainance supported	0%	100%	100%	0%	100%
Ability to create maintainance order	100%	100%	100%	100%	100%

ucts Flexibility MSP OE: 56% MSP SAP: 94% Pond.: 100% MMS OE: 56% MMS

Functionality	FSP OE	FSP SAP	Ponderation	OE Score	SAP S
Product configurator in manufacturing orders	50%	100%	100%	50%	100%
Multi-variants supports in product and BoM	50%	75%	100%	50%	75%
Multi unit of measures for the same product	100%	100%	100%	100%	100%
Product configurator in sales orders	25%	100%	100%	25%	100%

ity MSP OE: 50% MSP SAP: 100% Pond.: 100% MMS OE: 50% MMS

Functionality	FSP OE	FSP SAP	Ponderation	OE Score	SAP S
Quality in point per record in process	0%	100%	100%	0%	100%
Management of defective material	100%	100%	100%	100%	100%

rting MSP OE: 105% MSP SAP: 60% Pond.: 120% MMS OE: 88% MMS

Functionality	FSP OE	FSP SAP	Ponderation	OE Score	SAP S
Margins analysis on sales, products, manufacuting orders and	100%	100%	100%	100%	100%
Dynamic graphs on products and stock evolution	100%	25%	100%	100%	25%
Dynamic graphs on stocks forecasts	50%	50%	100%	50%	50%
Dynamic graphs on workcenter usage	100%	25%	100%	100%	25%

omain: **Project Management** DSP OE: 87% DSP SAP:

s-project and MSP OE: 80% MSP SAP: 100% Pond.: 100% MMS OE: 80% MMS
ct consolidation
ties

Functionality	FSP OE	FSP SAP	Ponderation	OE Score	SAP S
Template of projects and consolidation projects	75%	100%	100%	75%	100%
Sub-project nesting for collaborative project hierarchal	75%	100%	100%	75%	100%
Real-time status on tasks achievement	100%	100%	100%	100%	100%
Organisation of many project in one central place on web	100%	100%	100%	100%	100%
Prioritisation and dependencies between projects	50%	100%	100%	50%	100%

Project Management   DSP OE: 87% DSP SAP: 9∙

MSP OE:	100%	MSP SAP:	120%	Pond.:	100%	MMS OE:	100%	MMS SAP:

Functionality	FSP OE	FSP SAP	Ponderation	OE Score	SAP Score
Unlimited levels of project's structure	75%	100%	100%	75%	100%
Reorganisation of projects'structure in real time	100%	100%	100%	100%	100%
Multi unit of measures: hour/day/week/month	75%	100%	100%	75%	100%

MSP OE:	94%	MSP SAP:	100%	Pond.:	100%	MMS OE:	94%	MMS SAP:

Functionality	FSP OE	FSP SAP	Ponderation	OE Score	SAP Score
Creation of tasks based on sales orders	100%	100%	100%	100%	100%
Integration with the enterprise calendar	75%	100%	100%	75%	100%
Creation of tasks or projects based on manufacturing orders	100%	100%	100%	100%	100%
Integration between tasks and timesheets	100%	100%	100%	100%	100%

MSP OE:	100%	MSP SAP:	50%	Pond.:	100%	MMS OE:	100%	MMS SAP:

Functionality	FSP OE	FSP SAP	Ponderation	OE Score	SAP Score
SCRUM methodologies for IT companies	100%	50%	100%	100%	50%
Getting Things Done methodology	100%	50%	100%	100%	50%

MSP OE:	94%	MSP SAP:	110%	Pond.:	110%	MMS OE:	85%	MMS SAP:

Functionality	FSP OE	FSP SAP	Ponderation	OE Score	SAP Score
Financial indicators about profitability and invoicing	50%	100%	100%	50%	100%
Integration of projects with budgets	100%	100%	100%	100%	100%
Customers invoices forecasts based on projects	75%	100%	100%	75%	100%
Costs management including purchases, time of employee	100%	100%	100%	100%	100%
Supplier costs forecasts based on projects	100%	100%	100%	100%	100%

MSP OE:	110%	MSP SAP:	110%	Pond.:	110%	MMS OE:	100%	MMS SAP:

Functionality	FSP OE	FSP SAP	Ponderation	OE Score	SAP Score
Automatic invoicing based on time spent	100%	100%	100%	100%	100%
Automatic invoicing on fixed-price put on tasks	100%	100%	100%	100%	100%
Different rules for invoice price of costs, tasks or time	100%	100%	100%	100%	100%
Re-invoicing on costs on projects	100%	100%	100%	100%	100%

Project Management

DSP OE: 87% DSP SAP:

ect's Planning   MSP OE: 103%   MSP SAP: 110%   Pond.: 110%   MMS OE: 94%   MMS

Functionality	FSP OE	FSP SAP	Ponderation	OE Score	SAP S
Calendar view of tasks and deadlines	100%	100%	100%	100%	100
Short-term planning	100%	100%	100%	100%	100
Long-term planning	75%	100%	100%	75%	100
Gantt view of the plannings	100%	100%	100%	100%	100

orting   MSP OE: 80%   MSP SAP: 90%   Pond.: 100%   MMS OE: 80%   MMS

Functionality	FSP OE	FSP SAP	Ponderation	OE Score	SAP S
Availability of graphs based on tasks	100%	100%	100%	100%	100
Availability of graphs based on projects	100%	100%	100%	100%	100
Business Intelligence	0%	100%	100%	0%	100
Dashboards for projects managager	100%	75%	100%	100%	75
Dashboards for projects users	100%	75%	100%	100%	75

s organisation   MSP OE: 62%   MSP SAP: 110%   Pond.: 110%   MMS OE: 56%   MMS

Functionality	FSP OE	FSP SAP	Ponderation	OE Score	SAP S
Dynamic Perf chart manipulation	0%	100%	100%	0%	100
Report to display a gantt chart on multiple projects	75%	100%	100%	75%	100
Dynamic Gantt chart manipulation	75%	100%	100%	75%	100
Dynamic Calendar of tasks	75%	100%	100%	75%	100

d Party Integration   MSP OE: 88%   MSP SAP: 100%   Pond.: 100%   MMS OE: 88%   MMS

Functionality	FSP OE	FSP SAP	Ponderation	OE Score	SAP S
Integration with Outlook and Thunderbird	50%	100%	100%	50%	100
Document management to store information related to project	100%	100%	100%	100%	100
Automatic sends of emails based on tasks events	100%	100%	100%	100%	100
Automatic creation of tasks based on emails	100%	100%	100%	100%	100

Purchase Management

DSP OE: 79% DSP SAP:

matic propositions   MSP OE: 100%   MSP SAP: 100%   Pond.: 100%   MMS OE: 100%   MMS

urchases

Functionality	FSP OE	FSP SAP	Ponderation	OE Score	SAP S

Purchase Management

DSP OE: 79% DSP SAP: 97~

ropositions MSP OE: 100% MSP SAP: 100% Pond.: 100% MMS OE: 100% MMS SAP:

s

Functionality	FSP OE	FSP SAP	Ponderation	OE Score	SAP Score
Propositions based on minimum stock rules	100%	100%	100%	100%	100%
Recurring purchase orders support	100%	100%	100%	100%	100%
Propositions based on Master Production Schedule	100%	100%	100%	100%	100%
Propositions based on 'Make to Order' requirements	100%	100%	100%	100%	100%

ces MSP OE: 56% MSP SAP: 75% Pond.: 100% MMS OE: 56% MMS SAP:

Functionality	FSP OE	FSP SAP	Ponderation	OE Score	SAP Score
ISO9001 Suppliers evaluation	0%	0%	100%	0%	0%
Just-in-Time Support in Purchase Management	75%	100%	100%	75%	100%

ontrol MSP OE: 81% MSP SAP: 100% Pond.: 100% MMS OE: 81% MMS SAP:

Functionality	FSP OE	FSP SAP	Ponderation	OE Score	SAP Score
Reconciliation process	100%	100%	100%	100%	100%
Invoice control based on purchases	75%	100%	100%	75%	100%
Invoice control based on deliveries of services	75%	100%	100%	75%	100%
Invoice control based on deliveries of products	75%	100%	100%	75%	100%

agement MSP OE: 71% MSP SAP: 100% Pond.: 100% MMS OE: 71% MMS SAP:

Functionality	FSP OE	FSP SAP	Ponderation	OE Score	SAP Score
FIFO price support on products	0%	100%	100%	0%	100%
Sales prices can be automatically based on purchases prices	100%	100%	100%	100%	100%
End-of-year discount management	25%	100%	100%	25%	100%
Average price support per product	100%	100%	100%	100%	100%
Standard price support on products	100%	100%	100%	100%	100%
Supplier's pricelists and promotion support	100%	100%	100%	100%	100%

acilities MSP OE: 88% MSP SAP: 100% Pond.: 100% MMS OE: 88% MMS SAP:

Functionality	FSP OE	FSP SAP	Ponderation	OE Score	SAP Score
bility to link a purchase to a contract or an analytic account	100%	100%	100%	100%	100%
Open Purchase orders	100%	100%	100%	100%	100%
Ability to define recurring purchases	75%	100%	100%	75%	100%

Domain: **Purchase Management** DSP OE: 79% DSP SAP:

chases facilities MSP OE: 88% MSP SAP: 100% Pond.: 100% MMS OE: 88% MM

Functionality	FSP OE	FSP SAP	Ponderation	OE Score	SAP
Ability to define limitation of approval of quotes	100%	100%	100%	100%	10
Ability to define alerts on supplier purchase	100%	100%	100%	100%	10
Support for Request for Quotations	50%	100%	100%	50%	10

chases negotiation MSP OE: 42% MSP SAP: 100% Pond.: 100% MMS OE: 42% MM

Functionality	FSP OE	FSP SAP	Ponderation	OE Score	SAP
Purchase Tenders	25%	100%	100%	25%	10
Auction with suppliers	50%	100%	100%	50%	10
Public offers	50%	100%	100%	50%	10

orting MSP OE: 100% MSP SAP: 100% Pond.: 100% MMS OE: 100% MM

Functionality	FSP OE	FSP SAP	Ponderation	OE Score	SAP
Reports on suppliers purchases	100%	100%	100%	100%	10
Visibility in the RfQ: stocks, latests prices, supplier quality	100%	100%	100%	100%	10
Reports on suppliers quality	100%	100%	100%	100%	10

plier Portal on Web MSP OE: 92% MSP SAP: 100% Pond.: 100% MMS OE: 92% MM

Functionality	FSP OE	FSP SAP	Ponderation	OE Score	SAP
Ability to confirm availabilities of products	75%	100%	100%	75%	10
Ability to track received products	100%	100%	100%	100%	10
Ability to track invoices received and paid	100%	100%	100%	100%	10
Ability to put prices and/or confirm purchase orders	100%	100%	100%	100%	10
Ability to confirm delivery of products	75%	100%	100%	75%	10
Ability to track requests for quotations	100%	100%	100%	100%	10

Domain: **Sales Management** DSP OE: 92% DSP SAP:

omatic Invoicing MSP OE: 110% MSP SAP: 110% Pond.: 110% MMS OE: 100% MM

Functionality	FSP OE	FSP SAP	Ponderation	OE Score	SAP
Ability to generate invoices based on manufacturing orders	100%	100%	100%	100%	10
Ability to generate invoices based on tasks	100%	100%	100%	100%	10

n: **Sales Management** DSP OE: 92% DSP SAP: 1C

Invoicing MSP OE: 110% MSP SAP: 110% Pond.: 110% MMS OE: 100% MMS SAP:

Functionality	FSP OE	FSP SAP	Ponderation	OE Score	SAP Score
Ability to generate invoices based on deliveries	100%	100%	100%	100%	100%
Ability to generate invoices based on costs on project	100%	100%	100%	100%	100%
Ability to automatically generate draft or confirmed invoice	100%	100%	100%	100%	100%

on availability MSP OE: 100% MSP SAP: 100% Pond.: 100% MMS OE: 100% MMS SAP:

ations

Functionality	FSP OE	FSP SAP	Ponderation	OE Score	SAP Score
History of sales for the related customer	100%	100%	100%	100%	100%
Cost computation of the product based on quantities	100%	100%	100%	100%	100%
Zoom into the customer form in one click	100%	100%	100%	100%	100%
Theorical planning for manufacturing orders	100%	100%	100%	100%	100%
History of purchases for the selected product	100%	100%	100%	100%	100%
Future stock forecasts for selected product(s)	100%	100%	100%	100%	100%

MSP OE: 90% MSP SAP: 90% Pond.: 90% MMS OE: 100% MMS SAP:

Functionality	FSP OE	FSP SAP	Ponderation	OE Score	SAP Score
Support for advances invoices	100%	100%	100%	100%	100%
Ability to mix services, products and consumables in one sale	100%	100%	100%	100%	100%
Ability to select 'make to stock'/'make to order' logistics on	100%	100%	100%	100%	100%
Choose between invoice based on delivered or ordered	100%	100%	100%	100%	100%
Support for automatic invoice after delivery	100%	100%	100%	100%	100%
Ability to select the lot or tracking number on sale order line	100%	100%	100%	100%	100%

ale MSP OE: 77% MSP SAP: 100% Pond.: 100% MMS OE: 77% MMS SAP:

Functionality	FSP OE	FSP SAP	Ponderation	OE Score	SAP Score
integrate with third party peripherals	100%	100%	100%	100%	100%
Easy to use interface	100%	100%	100%	100%	100%
Able to send email and sms to customer	100%	100%	100%	100%	100%
Automatic generation of account entries	100%	100%	100%	100%	100%
capable to print receipts	100%	100%	100%	100%	100%

of Sale   MSP OE: 77%   MSP SAP: 100% Pond.:   100% MMS OE: 77% MMS

Functionality	FSP OE	FSP SAP	Ponderation	OE Score	SAP S
Multiple payment option	0%	100%	100%	0%	100%
centralize access of data	100%	100%	100%	100%	100%
Updated physical inventory details	100%	100%	100%	100%	100%
Integration with main module	100%	100%	100%	100%	100%
Product image available	0%	100%	100%	0%	100%
sale order creation	100%	100%	100%	100%	100%
Tax facility	100%	100%	100%	100%	100%
Touchscreen interface	0%	100%	100%	0%	100%

s and contracts   MSP OE: 95%   MSP SAP: 113%   Pond.:   110% MMS OE: 87% MMS

Functionality	FSP OE	FSP SAP	Ponderation	OE Score	SAP S
Support for FIFO costing method	0%	100%	100%	0%	100%
Unlimited number of pricelists	100%	100%	90%	100%	100%
Support for standard price costing method	100%	100%	100%	100%	100%
Support for LIFO costing method	0%	100%	110%	0%	100%
A pricelist can have an unlimitted number of versions	100%	100%	90%	100%	100%
Support for a pricelist system based on rules	100%	100%	100%	100%	100%
Prices can be based on any field of the product form	100%	100%	100%	100%	100%
Price computation using factors or sums	100%	100%	100%	100%	100%
Price can be computed based on others pricelist	100%	100%	100%	100%	100%
Multi-currencies support and automatic conversions	100%	100%	100%	100%	100%
Customer prices can be computed based cost of the product	100%	100%	90%	100%	100%
Customer prices can be computed based on supplier prices	100%	100%	90%	100%	100%
Support for average price costing method	100%	100%	100%	100%	100%

ations   MSP OE: 88%   MSP SAP: 100% Pond.:   100% MMS OE: 88% MMS

Functionality	FSP OE	FSP SAP	Ponderation	OE Score	SAP S
Only 2 fields to fill in to encode a quotation (partner, product)	100%	100%	90%	100%	100%

Sales Management

DSP OE: 92% DSP SAP: 10

MSP OE: 88% MSP SAP: 100% Pond.: 100% MMS OE: 88% MMS SAP:

Functionality	FSP OE	FSP SAP	Ponderation	OE Score	SAP Score
Ability to convert a quotation into a sale order	100%	100%	100%	100%	100%
Ability to create a quotation from a business opportunity	100%	100%	100%	100%	100%
Integration with document management system to store	100%	100%	100%	100%	100%
Support for attachment of files on quotations	100%	100%	100%	100%	100%
Support for versions of quotations	100%	100%	100%	100%	100%
While creating orders, the inventory for each item is available	100%	100%	110%	100%	100%
Drop Shipment Facility	0%	100%	100%	0%	100%

Warehouse Management

DSP OE: 85% DSP SAP: 9

upport MSP OE: 90% MSP SAP: 90% Pond.: 120% MMS OE: 75% MMS SAP:

Functionality	FSP OE	FSP SAP	Ponderation	OE Score	SAP Score
Barcode support for workcenters to track events	75%	75%	100%	75%	75%
Barcode support for receptions	75%	75%	100%	75%	75%
Barcode support for pickings	75%	75%	100%	75%	75%
Barcode support for manufacturing orders	75%	75%	100%	75%	75%

loves MSP OE: 100% MSP SAP: 100% Pond.: 100% MMS OE: 100% MMS SAP:

Functionality	FSP OE	FSP SAP	Ponderation	OE Score	SAP Score
Automatic propositions of internal pickings for manufacturing	100%	100%	100%	100%	100%

gement MSP OE: 75% MSP SAP: 92% Pond.: 100% MMS OE: 75% MMS SAP:

Functionality	FSP OE	FSP SAP	Ponderation	OE Score	SAP Score
Barcode support to encode and print lots labels	75%	75%	100%	75%	75%
Support for production lots (per product)	75%	100%	100%	75%	100%
Support for logistic lots (on palets and boxes)	75%	100%	100%	75%	100%

Inventories MSP OE: 100% MSP SAP: 100% Pond.: 100% MMS OE: 100% MMS SAP:

Functionality	FSP OE	FSP SAP	Ponderation	OE Score	SAP Score
Support for total and partial inventories	100%	100%	100%	100%	100%
Allows to continue working on products when doing an	100%	100%	100%	100%	100%

Warehouse Management
DSP OE: 85% DSP SAP: 92%

ucts   MSP OE: 75%   MSP SAP: 100%   Pond.: 100%   MMS OE: 75%   MMS

Functionality	FSP OE	FSP SAP	Ponderation	OE Score	SAP S
Facility of Non-stock items	100%	100%	100%	100%	100
Support for variants with multiple dimensions	50%	100%	100%	50%	100
Support for variants with one dimension	50%	100%	100%	50%	100
Visibility of real stock and future stocks in product's form	100%	100%	100%	100%	100

ucts Routes   MSP OE: 60%   MSP SAP: 80%   Pond.: 80%   MMS OE: 75%   MMS

Functionality	FSP OE	FSP SAP	Ponderation	OE Score	SAP S
Manage product's route in manufacturing chains	75%	100%	100%	75%	100
Manage long delays in product's routes (seas/oceans/ports)	25%	100%	100%	25%	100
Manage product's route in the warehouse	75%	100%	100%	75%	100
Unlimitted number of locations for a warehouse	100%	100%	100%	100%	100
Locations defined in a hierarchy structure, with unlimited	100%	100%	100%	100%	100

ing Products   MSP OE: 100%   MSP SAP: 120%   Pond.: 120%   MMS OE: 83%   MMS

Functionality	FSP OE	FSP SAP	Ponderation	OE Score	SAP S
Planification of stock based on receptions of the product	75%	100%	100%	75%	100
Manages products to be rent	75%	100%	100%	75%	100
Manages stock at customer location	100%	100%	100%	100%	100

eability   MSP OE: 100%   MSP SAP: 94%   Pond.: 100%   MMS OE: 100%   MMS

Functionality	FSP OE	FSP SAP	Ponderation	OE Score	SAP S
Graphical upstream traceability graph or tree	100%	75%	100%	100%	75
Traceability on logistic units (on palets/boxes)	100%	100%	100%	100%	100
Traceability on manufactured lots (on products)	100%	100%	100%	100%	100
Tracebility up to the customer or supplier locations	100%	100%	100%	100%	100

ehouse Organisation   MSP OE: 83%   MSP SAP: 67%   Pond.: 100%   MMS OE: 83%

Functionality	FSP OE	FSP SAP	Ponderation	OE Score	SAP S
Graphical representation of zones according to products usage	100%	0%	100%	100%	0
Capacity management per location and product	50%	100%	100%	50%	100
Builtin interface with automated racks	100%	100%	100%	100%	100